NEW TESTAMENT ESSAYS

VINCENT TAYLOR

New Testament Essays

WILLIAM B. EERDMANS PUBLISHING COMPANY
Grand Rapids, Michigan

Foreword

THE Revd Dr. Vincent Taylor was accepted into the ministry of the Methodist Church in 1906. He received his theological training at Richmond College, Surrey, and gained his B.D. degree and also the B.D. Honours Degree at London University. His first book on *The Historical Evidence for the Virgin Birth* gained for him the Ph.D., and the degree of D.D. was awarded in recognition of his book, *Behind the Third Gospel*, in which he worked out in detail what has become known as the Proto-Luke Theory. His high standing in the world of New Testament scholarship was recognized by his appointment as Tutor in New Testament studies at Headingley College, Leeds, in 1930, and six years later he was appointed Principal. This position he held with great distinction until his retirement in 1953. Both during his teaching career and also in his retirement he wrote many important books, some on New Testament subjects, others on Theology, and still others of a more elementary type for the general reader, the lay preacher and students. In 1933 his book on *The Formation of the Gospel Tradition* provided the first introduction for many English readers to the new approach to the Gospels known as 'Form Criticism'. Then came his famous trilogy on the Atonement—*Jesus and His Sacrifice, The Atonement in New Testament Teaching, Forgiveness and Reconciliation*. More recently he delivered the Speaker's Lectures at Oxford and these appeared as a further trilogy on the Person of Christ—*The Names of Jesus, The Life and Ministry of Jesus*, and *The Person of Christ in New Testament Teaching*. In 1952 appeared his magnificent commentary on *The Gospel according to St. Mark*. In 1956 he spent several months at Drew University as visiting lecturer, and a special series of lectures delivered there have been published under the title, *The Cross of Christ*. Several

Universities, including Glasgow, Leeds, and Dublin, have awarded him the honorary D.D., and a still further honour was conferred upon him when he was made a Fellow of the British Association. Dr. Taylor died in November 1968.

The papers in this volume were written over many years and indeed one of them goes back to the days of Dr. Taylor's Methodist Circuit ministry. Mr. George's tribute was given at the funeral service and Dr. Mitton's essay was specially written for this collection.

Contents

Vincent Taylor

by A. Raymond George

VINCENT TAYLOR was a Methodist preacher, a scholar-preacher, one whose scholarship was never merely academic but always at the service of preaching.

He was trained at Richmond College, for which he retained a great affection. He once said that the most useful of all his books was Moulton-Geden's *Concordance*; its preface shows that most of it was written at Richmond. Trained at a College with a great tradition of biblical scholarship, he must surely have caught some of his inspiration there. He did not have great educational advantages before he went there. It is remarkable that he who later was rightly honoured by so many Universities was not himself taught at a University, for Richmond was not then closely linked with the University of London, as it is now. Nor did he obtain a degree while he was there; he took the ordinary course. But after he had left, working externally amid the many duties of a Circuit Minister, he obtained by his own efforts his degrees: B.D., Ph.D., D.D. At this time he suffered from a serious illness. But he had a great faith that God intended him for some special work; and so he came through it.

He was always a very hard worker. He wrote his books by the discipline of writing at least a page each day. Once he was sent a book in German to review. At that time he knew no German; but he did not admit that. He bought a German grammar, and thus learnt German and reviewed the book at the same time. He was unequalled in his conscientious and meticulous attention to detail. And all this was combined for many years with the duties of Principal and Resident Tutor of Wesley College, Headingley.

The seed thus sown bore fruit, particularly in his books. He was a prolific writer, and when we record four great contri-

1

butions which he made we shall still have left out several books, including some textbooks very useful for students.

First, there was his contribution to Source-criticism, in which he dealt with the sources behind St. Luke's Gospel. Second, at a time when very little was generally known in this country about Form-criticism, he virtually introduced it to English readers, explaining it and also making critical comments on it, in *The Formation of the Gospel Tradition*. Then, thirdly, he turned to New Testament theology; he would have been the first to say that the study of Introduction is indispensable, but after giving so much time to questions of Introduction, he wanted to consider what the New Testament actually says. And so came the great trilogy on the Atonement, and another shorter book on the same theme later on. Afterwards there came yet another trilogy, that on the Person of Christ. But, fourthly, in between the two trilogies, he turned to writing a commentary, and so came the great commentary on St. Mark, which will surely be a standard work for many years to come. He said at that time that writing a commentary was different from writing his earlier books. In them he had said what he wanted to say on the themes that interested him. 'Now', he said, 'I have to write about every verse, whether it specially interests me or not'. But such a challenge was just what appealed to his disciplined mind, and there were few verses on which he did not find something worthwhile to say.

It is difficult to assess this volume of work, and opinions may vary as to his greatest contribution. It perhaps lay in *Jesus and His Sacrifice* and in his Fernley-Hartley Lecture *The Atonement in New Testament Teaching*. In these he rescued the doctrine of sacrifice from the disregard into which because of its abuses it had in some circles fallen; and then, saying that sacrifice is a category of representation, he went on to outline a doctrine of the Work of Christ in representative and vicarious terms.

But his contribution to the kenotic or self-emptying theory of the Person of Christ was also of great importance, and systematic theologians cannot lecture for long on either the Person or the Work of Christ without referring to his contributions, just as their New Testament colleagues refer to his works in that field. It was moreover these themes which drew him out as a preacher. Two most memorable sermons of his had as their texts 'He emptied himself' and 'He pleased not himself'. And among his favourite quotations were these lines from Charles Wesley, whom he often quoted, lines with which he finished *Jesus and His Sacrifice*.

> *He pleads His passion on the tree,*
> *He shows Himself to God for me.*

Now the fruit which he thus bore became as it were a fresh seed bearing a further harvest. For one thing his books brought him recognition: his honorary degrees, his Fellowship of the British Academy, the Burkitt medal. They brought him the esteem of his own Church. The greatness of his achievement was perhaps not always fully grasped, but certainly Methodists were proud of him. He had also a great influence in other denominations. When the great Anglican liturgical scholar Gregory Dix was dying, he had lost all interest even in reading paperback detective stories or in talking to other people, and then someone gave him Dr. Taylor's newly-published commentary on St. Mark. As he looked at it, his interest was aroused; he read it eagerly, and received fresh energy, so that he was stimulated to resume conversation with another patient, and actually led him to Christ. A few hours later Gregory Dix died. His brother wrote to Vincent Taylor, full of gratitude. Dr. Taylor related the incident in a sermon, but with characteristic modesty said little of his own part in it, never making it clear that it was his own book which was involved. But to his colleagues he told the whole story, humbly grateful that his book had been used in this unusual and indirect way in the conversion of a man to Christ.

Another part of the harvest which came from his sowing lay in the encouragement which he gave to younger scholars, such as Dr. Leslie Mitton and Mr. Owen Evans. For many years Dr. Taylor helped the Editors of the *Expository Times* with his advice; he encouraged others to write for it and probably wrote himself many of the anonymous paragraphs which stand at the beginning of it. The appointment of Dr. Mitton as Editor when the Hastings family retired thus carried on the tradition.

In a sense Dr. Taylor's own ministry was the fruit of his scholarship. He was Minister in several Circuits before he went to Headingley, and he also had a Circuit during the second world war. These Circuits reaped the fruit of his preaching. His whole life at Headingley was part of this harvest. The first impression which he gave to colleagues or to students there was one of a certain austerity; this arose from his own high standards. He did so much that he was a difficult man even to try to keep up with. But as one got to know him better, and enjoyed the gracious fellowship which he extended in his home with Mrs. Taylor, then austerity gave way to sympathy and friendship, which in turn elicited affection.

All this sprang of course from his own deep faith. As he was among other things an author, let him speak for himself. At the end of the last chapter of the last book of the trilogy on the *Person of Christ* he says:

'Faith alone knows who Jesus is. This demand for faith is wrongly conceived if we imagine that we can short-circuit the issue by neglecting the study of Scripture and the fellowship of the Church, for while God speaks to us directly by His Spirit, He speaks also through His Word and through the life of the Christian community. Faith is the response to this threefold witness. Only when this response is made do we learn the truth of the words addressed to Thomas, "Because thou hast seen me, thou hast believed; blessed are they that have not seen, and have believed." Then only do we cry, "My Lord and my God".'

Vincent Taylor: New Testament Scholar

by C. L. Mitton

FOR MORE than thirty years the name of Vincent Taylor has been honoured throughout the world as that of one of the most outstanding New Testament scholars of our time. In recognition of his scholarship many honours have been accorded him. Among these were his appointment as a Fellow of the British Association and the award of the Burkitt Medal and his election to the office of President of the Society for New Testament Studies, a society whose membership is drawn from New Testament scholars from all over the world. His first D.D. was awarded to him by London University on the basis of a thesis, and honorary Doctorates of Divinity were later added by the Universities of Leeds, Dublin, and Glasgow. Special invitations led to his delivering series of lectures at many Universities including those of Oxford and Cambridge, Drew and New Jersey. When the *Expository Times* printed a sequence of articles on 'Theologians of Our Time' (later, in 1966, published by T. & T. Clark in book form) his name was one of those included. His output of scholarly books was remarkable. Out of the total of fifteen books which he wrote, eleven were major contributions to scholarship, the others being text books for students, or study books for Church laymen.

If for thirty years he was respected throughout the world as a great scholar, in the story of the Methodist Church he must be recognized as one of the very greatest that Church has ever produced, and one of whom the whole Church can be justly proud.

All these achievements would have been extraordinary, even if Dr. Taylor had started life with the most favourable of educational opportunities, and continued in later life to work in University appointments, with the leisure for study and writing which these are designed to afford. But Vincent Taylor enjoyed neither of these advantages. A period of secular employment followed his schooldays, and his 'higher' education did not begin until, at the age of twenty-two, he went to the Methodist theological college at Richmond, Surrey, as an accepted candidate for the Ministry of the Methodist Church. It was not, however, until two years after leaving college that he took the B.D. of London University as an external student, proceeding a few years later to the B.D. Honours in New Testament Studies, a step which opened the way to the higher degrees. There followed in due course the Ph.D. and D.D. of London University, both awarded on the basis of theses, which were also published as books. Then came the long sequence of distinguished theological publications, starting in 1920 and continuing till 1961. He continued, in fact, to work until 1965 on a book dealing with the Lukan Passion Narrative, which is not yet published.

All this was achieved in spite of the severe educational disadvantages of his early days. It was achieved also against the background of a busy life as a Methodist Minister, in Circuit work from 1909 to 1930 and then as a College Tutor at Headingley College, Leeds till his retirement in 1953. This later appointment involved not only a full time-table of teaching New Testament subjects, but also, from 1936, the responsibility of the Principalship, which included oversight of the discipline and corporate life of the College, as well as the administration of the College buildings. For most men this combination of duties would have left neither time nor energy for research and writing. This makes Dr. Taylor's scholarly and literary achievements all the more remarkable. These, in spite of his splendid qualities of mind, were made possible only by a most rigorous self-discipline, astonishing powers of concentration and a relentless stewardship of time.

His books remain the chief monument of his industry and his scholarly discernment. All bear the mark of exhaustive thoroughness, patient attention to every detail, and pene-trating critical acumen. Unmistakably present is also a deep reverence for the person of Christ. This sprang not only from his own personal devotion to Christ, but also from the objective fact that the whole of the New Testament without any dis-sentient note bears witness to the unique significance of Jesus.

Both these qualities of critical perception and humble devotion to Christ are noticeably present in his first published work on the bases of which he was awarded the degree of Ph.D. This was *The Historical Evidence for the Virgin Birth*, published by the Oxford University Press in 1920. It is a measure of the intrinsic worth of the book that so distinguished a Press accepted it, though the writer was at the time quite unknown.

The aim of the book is not to determine whether or not the Church has been right in claiming that Jesus was born of a virgin, but the preliminary task of finding out how far the New Testament itself affirms this doctrine and insists on its importance. With scrupulous impartiality he examined every passage in the New Testament which has ever been appealed to as providing support for the doctrine, and subjected them all to the most careful scrutiny and critical appraisal. The conclusion he reached in the end is one which few scholars would dissent from today. It was that only two of all the books in the New Testament explicitly affirm the Virgin Birth as a fact. These are Matthew and Luke. Supposed references in other books are all less than explicit. He recognized also that a distinction could be made between the witness of Matthew and Luke, in that the doctrine is integral to the nativity stories as recorded by Matthew, but it appears in Luke only in phrases which are in a sense detachable: an extreme critic might in fact argue that they are not part of the original form of the Gospel, though there is no literary evidence to support such a claim.

From a purely literary point of view, therefore, the evidence of the New Testament was inconclusive, and Dr. Taylor's final judgement was that theological considerations must decide the issue. Some readers felt disappointed that the matter was left like this. They felt that the whole trend of the investigation had raised difficulties for the acceptance of the doctrine rather than provided strong reasons for substantiating it. If twenty-five of the twenty-seven books in the New Testament ignored it, this suggested that the writers either did not know or did not accept the doctrine; certainly it meant they did not regard it as an indispensable factor in the Christian Faith. Moreover the Matthaean narrative, where the doctrine receives its firmest support from within the New Testament, belongs to the narrative material which is peculiar to Matthew and, from the point of view of historicity, this is the least reliable material in the synoptic tradition. The investigation of the historical evidence, therefore, had seemed to cast doubt on the doctrine rather than provide verification of it, even though it was firmly embedded in the Creed and could claim the support of two New Testament writers.

What did Dr. Taylor mean by saying that the final decision rested on theological factors? He meant that purely historical investigation could not determine the truth about the real nature of Christ. The New Testament writers without the slightest hint of dissent declare that in Jesus Christ God had made Himself uniquely present in and available to human life. This was a theological judgement, not a historical one. Different writers express in different ways the uniqueness of Jesus in this relation to God: titles such as Son of God, Image of God, the Logos and others are called into service. But of the uniqueness there is complete unanimity and exponents of the New Testament believed that it justified them in affirming the Church's confession of His divinity or deity. Dr. Taylor himself accepted as true this unvaried testimony of the New Testament. The further theological question then arose: could God indeed make Himself so uniquely present in a human life except by means of a birth fundamentally different from a normal birth? If theologically the 'divinity' of Christ required a virgin birth, then the historical evidence was not sufficient to deny a virgin birth. If theologically a virgin birth was not required, the historical evidence was not such as to compel belief in it. On this theological question Dr. Taylor did not pretend to make a decision. The historical evidence was his prescribed area of study, and theological considerations lay beyond his self-imposed limits. He did not doubt the uniqueness of Jesus, but the further question whether this uniqueness required a virgin birth, lay beyond his field of enquiry. He was content to analyse what was said in the New Testament about it, and his book remains the definitive treatment of this subject.

His next book came six years later in 1926. It was *Behind the Third Gospel* and was the thesis on which he was awarded the degree of D.D. by London University. This was a detailed, critical study of certain literary features of the Third Gospel, and a careful presentation of a newly-suggested solution of the problem they posed.

For many years the focus of interest in the study of the synoptic Gospels had been the literary relationship between them. The most widely accepted explanation of their inter-relationship was what had come to be called 'The Two Document Hypothesis'. The heart of the problem lay in two acknowledged facts: (i) that the material in Mark was largely found also in both Matthew and Luke, and (ii) that Matthew and Luke also contained a considerable amount of material in common, which was not shared by Mark. Older theories had assumed that this was to be explained on the grounds that Luke and Mark had used Matthew. Scholars had, however, demonstrated the insuperable difficulties of such a solution, and in general they had reached agreement that in fact it was Mark which was the earliest of the three Gospels, and that Matthew and Luke had both derived large sections of their Gospels from Mark. In addition, it was claimed that there must have been some other document (now lost) from which Matthew and Luke had taken the non-Markan material they held in common. This 'document' came to be known, for convenience, as 'Q'. The currently accepted solution of the synoptic problem was that before Matthew and Luke wrote their Gospels two documents, Mark and Q, were already in existence and it was the common use of these two documents which accounted for the large degree of material shared by Matthew and Luke. The close similarity in the actual words used and in the order of episodes recorded was believed to preclude any explanation based merely on the use of oral traditions.

In October 1921 Canon B. H. Streeter in an article in the *Hibbert Journal* suggested a refinement of this theory, which was later amplified in his book *The Four Gospels*. He pointed out a striking difference between the ways Matthew and Luke had used their two sources. Matthew clearly used Mark as his framework, and reproduced almost the whole of it. His method was to take passages which dealt with a common theme from Mark, Q and his own special material and with extraordinary skill weave them all together into a most carefully blended whole, all three sources being in many places interwoven together. Luke had acted differently. He combined Q and his own material, weaving them together as Matthew had done. But he had treated the Markan material quite differently. It was never interwoven with the other sources, but always kept separate by itself, unmixed with other material, and simply inserted as Markan blocks at chosen points into the other conflated sections. This suggested to Streeter that Luke had not in fact used Mark as his basic document, but had first blended Q with his own special material (called 'L') and only at a later stage became acquainted with Mark. Selections from the Markan material had then been inserted into the first draft of the gospel which he had already written. This earlier draft of the gospel Streeter called 'Proto-Luke'.

Dr. Taylor sensed the importance of this brilliant suggestion, but wished to subject it to the most exhaustive tests to determine whether it could be accepted with confidence as the valid explanation of the phenomena in question. His book *Behind the Third Gospel* is the record of his investigations which left him fully convinced that Streeter's insight was in fact demonstrably correct and that Mark did not provide the basic structure of Luke's Gospel but was rather 'a quarry from which stone was obtained to enlarge an already existing building'. He remained convinced, to the very end of his life, that this theory explained better than any other the literary facts he found in Luke's Gospel. He did not claim that Proto-Luke had ever been published, only that Luke had concluded a 'first draft' of his Gospel before inserting Markan material into it. Moreover he fully recognized that in the Passion narrative Luke had been more flexible, and here had incorporated Markan material in a somewhat less rigid way. Indeed the Passion narrative may well have had to be rewritten entirely in the light of Mark. Even in the Passion narrative, however, he believed it could be demonstrated that the tradition on which Luke primarily depended was not that of Mark, but a non-Markan original which had been amplified with Markan material.

One of the arguments in favour of Proto-Luke was that though the Markan insertions, when read in sequence, did not make a continuous story, the non-Markan material did.

To provide the means by which readers could conveniently test this for themselves he published in 1927 a pamphlet entitled *The First Draft of Luke's Gospel*, which was the third Gospel with the Markan elements removed. He believed that anyone, reading this through continuously, would be persuaded of what he claimed.

The Proto-Luke theory has not gained the same measure of acceptance as the Two Document theory has achieved. Many scholars of the highest standing have been convinced of its truth for example, Dodd, T. W. Manson, Jeremias, Grant,— R. H. Fuller; and two German scholars, F. Rehkopf and H. Schurmann, have independently argued for a non-Markan tradition as the basis behind the Lukan Passion narrative. There are others, however, who have remained unpersuaded, though they have been curiously reluctant to specify their arguments against it, preferring to speak vaguely of Markan influences discernible in the supposedly non-Markan sections. Perhaps the fullest statement in opposition to it is to be found in Kummell's *Introduction to the New Testament* (Eng. Tr. 1966; pp. 92–95). To offset this G. B. Caird in his distinguished commentary on St. Luke in the Pelican series (pp. 23–27) not only vigorously presents old and new arguments in favour of Proto-Luke, but regards the case for it as fully established.

Dr. Taylor's book is primarily concerned with the hypothesis of Proto-Luke as the best way of explaining the literary features of the Third Gospel. When, however, this had been established, as he believed, by cumulative arguments, he added two concluding chapters, one on the value of the hypothesis, if true, and the other on the Theology of Proto-Luke. Its value lies in the isolation of a document which may be dated about the same time as Mark's Gospel—or even earlier, since it was already in existence before Mark came to Luke's notice. Dr. Taylor summarizes his points in these words: 'We have good reason to trust it as an early and reliable historical work . . . It is certainly a first-class authority comparable to Mark . . . It is an added help to the critic who above all else desires to cut the highway for true historical progress' (p. 254). Its theological value springs also in part from its early date. Against those who had argued that Luke's theological position was merely a reflection of what was found in Paul's letters, the isolation of Proto-Luke and the early date required for it placed this document 'almost within the life-time of the Apostle Paul' (p. 274). In so far, therefore, as it echoes Pauline ideas about the Gospel Message, the explanation is, not that Paul speaks through Luke, but Christ Himself speaks (both in Luke and through Paul). 'The Proto-Luke Hypothesis . . . throws back into the earliest stage of Gospel tradition the picture of a Christ whose compassion blesses the outcast of society, and whose last words to man are a message of hope to a dying thief.'

If the Proto-Luke hypothesis ever wins its way into scholarly orthodoxy, it will be due to Streeter's flash of insight and Vincent Taylor's patient and detailed demonstration of its validity—what Dr. Taylor himself called his 'substantial verification' of it.

The publication of Dr. Taylor's next book in 1930 coincided with his appointment to the Chair of New Testament Studies at Wesley College, Leeds, after twenty years in the Circuit work of the Methodist Church. It was an appropriate publication for the occasion, because it was a text-book for students called *The Gospels: A Short Introduction* (Epworth Press). This showed the author in a new, but not unexpected, light. It revealed his great skill as a teacher. As a text-book it was altogether admirable. One could hardly imagine a better— clear, concise, orderly and balanced. In 120 pages he put before the reader all the main facts and theories needed to give him in short compass an adequate introduction to the Gospels. A fourth and enlarged edition was called for in 1938, and still the demand for it did not flag. In 1960 a ninth edition had to be printed to keep up with the persistent demand. It was right up to date and covered even the most recent of important contributions to scholarship. In 1930 'Form-criticism', though already a storm-centre of theological dispute in Germany, had hardly been heard of in this country, except by scholars. But in this book the whole of the second chapter, (entitled 'The Earliest Tradition'), was devoted to this subject and here readers were introduced briefly but sympathetically to 'the form critical method' and tribute was paid to 'Bultmann's keen-sighted analysis' of the Gospel materials. There were indeed also warnings, lest readers be swept off their feet in uncritical adulation of the new and unproved hypotheses. Dr. Taylor refused, for instance, to accept Bultmann's classification of certain incidents as 'the work of the community' (as, for instance, 'The Plucking of the Ears of Corn'), or as 'ideal scenes' (as 'The Widow's Mite'). This somewhat high-handed way of dismissing the historicity of these materials on the basis of a subjective judgement rather than logical demonstration he regarded as quite unjustifiable. His guarded approach to this new field of research illustrates both Dr. Taylor's quick openness to new ideas, and at the same time his refusal to allow newness or current fashion to hypnotize his critical faculty.

His deep interest in Form-criticism as a new method of Gospel-study led to the writing of his next book: *The Formation of the Gospel Tradition* (Macmillan, 1933), based on a series of public lectures at the University of Leeds. At this time there was hardly anything written in Britain about this new approach. Bultmann's *Die Geschichte der synoptischen Tradition* had appeared in its second edition, but this, as also the works of Albertz, Dibelius, Fascher, and Schmidt, was available only in German. For a great many English-speaking students this book of Dr. Taylor's was their first introduction to Form-criticism, and they were fortunate, because it was a very shrewd book, full of wise guidance. On the continent Form-criticism, under the influence of Bultmann's extreme radicalism, quickly became largely identified with extreme scepticism about the historical value of the Gospel materials. The Gospels were interpreted as representing only the faith of those who compiled them. Dr. Taylor studied all these German writers with interest and sympathy, but with his characteristic caution declined to follow them when they stepped beyond analysis and demonstration to speculation.

Dibelius is given the credit of being the 'pathfinder' in this new enterprise, and his more careful approach is preferred to Bultmann's over-confidence in the new method. Bultmann's brilliant scholarship, however, is generously acknowledged: 'It is impossible to doubt the importance of his work and the influence it will exert on the study of the gospels.' The twenty-five years since that statement have proved the accuracy of this forecast. At the same time he regretted the 'sceptical

direction' of Bultmann's studies, and insisted that 'this was
not the necessary trend of the method', but only the direction
which Bultmann's highly individual approach had given to it.
While admiring Bultmann's scholarship, he questioned his
judgement in this matter. Somewhat caustically he writes:
'The real charge against him is that he is kinder to the
possibilities than to the probabilities . . . It would not be unfair
to describe his work as a study of the cult of the conceivable.'

Dr. Taylor's book was not only a presentation and co-
ordination of the recent researches of German scholars; in it he
himself made his own solid contribution to the subject. The
students at Wesley College, Leeds, at that time remember how
he enlisted their co-operation to test the effect of oral tradition
on the material transmitted. He read a story to a small group of
men, who in turn told it to others, who passed it on to others.
At each stage the form of the story was recorded, and the
changes taking place in the transmission were carefully
analysed. The results of this practical investigation are recorded
on p. 124 of his book and the investigation itself is described
in Appendix B, pp. 202–209. It led to illuminating conclusions.
Chief among them perhaps was the incontrovertible fact that
though, in the process of transmission, details such as names
were often omitted or changed the main thrust of the episode
remained intact.

His presentation of the researches of the German scholars
was most valuable. He listed the different 'forms' which had
been identified, and indicated how the same 'form' had—most
confusingly—been given different names by different scholars.
What Dibelius called *Paradigmen*, Bultmann named *Apophthegmata*; Dibelius's *Novellen* were the same as Bultmann's
'Miracle Stories'; Dibelius used *Mythen* for what Bultmann
called *Legenda*. Perhaps it is at this point that Dr. Taylor has
left his own mark most decisively on this area of research. The
names *Paradigmen* and *Apophthegmata* were used to describe the
short stylized narratives whose main purpose was to lead up to
a memorable saying (a kind of 'punch-line') at the end. Neither
of these German words was really descriptive of this form.
Paradigmen means 'models', and *Apophthegmata* means 'pointed
sayings'. Dr. Taylor suggested a far more suitable name. He
called them 'Pronouncement Stories'. This name does justice

both to the narrative element in this 'form' of the tradition and to the pronouncement at the end. It has been widely accepted by others. Professor R. H. Fuller, for instance, in *A Critical Introduction to the New Testament* (Duckworth, 1966, p. 85) writes: 'Taylor's term, "pronouncement stories" is to be preferred, for it gives equal weight to the scene and the saying.'

Dr. Taylor does not doubt that the material preserved in this form, as in others, was remembered and used because of its value to the Christian community that treasured it. But he totally rejects Bultmann's claim that many of them were, in fact, 'created' (invented) by the community in order to provide answers to some of its own problems. Pertinently he asks: 'If the stories are the products of Christian imagination, why do they not increase in number as time passes, and as new problems confront the growing Church?' He quotes Albertz who wrote, concerning those Pronouncement Stories which report Jesus in conflict with His enemies: 'It is the historical Jesus who is attacked, not the Christ on whom the community believed' (p. 87). He adds: 'Far from acquiescing in any denial of the historical element in these stories, we ought rather to esteem them among the strongest and most stable elements in the Gospel tradition'.

The Form Critical method he welcomed for the many insights it provided for understanding the Gospels and the process by which they had been compiled, but the claim that these methods undermined belief in the substantial historicity of the Gospels he totally rejected.

Those who knew Dr. Taylor personally knew how important to him was the Death of Christ. This was due not merely to a private conviction of its central significance for Christian Faith, but far more to the fact that it looms so large in the New Testament, not least in the Gospels. Indeed the Gospels have been described as Passion narratives extended backwards. In consequence Dr. Taylor immediately sensed the inadequacy of any theological system which failed to do justice to the centrality of the Cross or interpreted its mysterious power in Christian history as little more than its ability to bring individual men and women to penitence and holiness. He was keenly aware that the Cross, as it was presented in the New Testament, possessed cosmic significance. It was, therefore, no

surprise to his friends when his researches turned towards this
focal point of Christian devotion.

For twenty-five years he had concentrated his studies of the
New Testament, and especially the Gospels, on issues in-
volving mainly literary and historical questions. He believed
strongly in the necessity of this 'critical' approach as a preparation for the more important study of the theological
content of the New Testament. He was suspicious of the
competence of those who plunged straight into theological
expositions without having prepared the way first by dis-
sciplined, critical study of the materials with which they
were working. But he himself had now served a long and
thorough apprenticeship to the critical method and felt ready
to turn to the issue which constitutes the supreme importance
of the New Testament—its teaching about Christ. The preface
of his next book opened with this sentence: 'After devoting
something like twenty-five years to the study of the problems
of literary and historical criticism in connection with the
Gospels, and especially the minutiae of source criticism, I am
conscious of a strong desire to investigate some more vital
issue, arising out of these studies, which bears intimately
upon Christian life and practice.'

He set himself, therefore, to analyse and expound what the
Death of Christ meant for the New Testament writers, and
the theme of his first book on this subject was the attitude of
Jesus Himself to His death, as far as this can be discerned in
the Gospels. The title of the book tells us not only its subject,
but something also of the writer's conclusions about it. Not
many Nonconformist scholars of that time would have chosen
to call one of their books *Jesus and His Sacrifice* (Macmillan).
But for Dr. Taylor the word 'sacrifice' was the word best fitted
to express the meaning of the Cross which emerged from his
studies.

The book starts with a thorough examination of Old Testament antecedents, since 'the thought of Jesus is steeped in
that of the Old Testament and cannot be understood apart
from it.' The next section deals with all the sayings found on
the lips of Jesus which have reference to His Death. It is noted
that in the Synoptic tradition these are found oddly enough,
only in Mark and 'L', not at all in 'M' and 'Q'. The words of

Jesus at the Last Supper, as Paul reports them in I Corinthians 11; 23–5, are also included. The Johannine sayings are treated separately. Dr. Taylor does not uncritically accept the historicity of the sayings, and each one is discussed from this point of view before its meaning and implications are drawn out. When the whole of the material has been thoroughly scrutinized, the emphases which keep on recurring and so may be claimed to be characteristic of the thought of Jesus are then listed. This summary has in fact exercised considerable influence on many readers of the book and may usefully be noted here:

i. The belief of Jesus that the purpose of His Passion 'lay deep in the Providence of God'.

ii. Implied in it is a relationship between Jesus and the Father 'of perfect unity'.

iii. Jesus understood His death to be 'an active element in His Messianic vocation'.

iv. His Passion is closely connected with the Kingdom of God.

v. It represents 'a victorious struggle with the powers of evil'.

vi. His suffering is both 'representative and vicarious'.

vii. It involves a close personal relationship between Himself and sinners.

viii. He intended men to participate in His self-offering and to appropriate the power of His surrendered life.

ix. It is 'an activity which in some measure men can reproduce'.

Dr. Taylor set himself to discover a 'unifying principle' which runs through and holds together these nine recurring features, and he finds it in 'the sacrificial principle'. Sacrifice must, however, be liberated from any idea of 'appeasing an angry God'. The essence and aim of sacrifice, as it is applicable to what Jesus did on the Cross, is to restore fellowship by means of a representative offering, which, however, is closely co-ordinated with 'the attitude of the worshipper'.

Then in the last chapter Dr. Taylor seeks to derive from his studies of the words of Jesus some abiding principles, on the basis of which a worthy understanding of the Atonement for today can be worked out. He pays tribute to the enduring truths within the Abelardian theory (sometimes called 'The Moral Influence Theory'), but insists that by themselves they are inadequate. The Cross does more than awaken penitence in the sinner and stimulate his desire for goodness. Indeed there is very little of this particular emphasis in these Gospel sayings. Rather they point to what is commonly called an 'objective' theory of the Atonement. The perfect obedience of Jesus to the Father, His perfect submission to the judgement of God upon sin, His self-offering as the expression of His perfect penitence for the sins of men—all this has transformed the relationship between man and God. The chapter closes with the quotation, which poignantly makes this point:

> *He pleads His passion on the tree,*
> *He shows Himself to God for me.*

This book proved to be the first of a trilogy on the Atonement. The second followed quickly in 1940, *The Atonement in New Testament Teaching*. It was delivered as the Fernley-Hartley Lecture at the Methodist Conference, and so was published by the Epworth Press. It did for the rest of the New Testament what the first had done for the sayings of Jesus. It analysed what each writer had thought about the Death of Jesus, and then picked out those recurring emphases which could be said to be characteristic of the over-all attitude of the New Testament. On the basis of this analysis the final chapter seeks to formulate a modern restatement of the doctrine of the Atonement. It must, he concludes, do justice to the following truths, constantly reiterated in the New Testament:

i. The Atonement is the Work of God, as He restores sinners to fellowship with Himself.
ii. It both reveals *and* expresses His love for men.
iii. It is accomplished through the work of Christ, whose suffering is vicarious, representative, and sacrificial in character.
iv. The Atonement is consummated in the experience of men through faith-union with Christ, through sacramental communion with Him and in sacrificial living and suffering.

The third book in the trilogy appeared in 1941. It was *Forgiveness and Reconciliation*, published by Macmillan. It was a careful and exhaustive study of such themes in the New Testament as forgiveness, reconciliation, and justification in their relation to the Death of Christ. Dr. Taylor acknowledged that in modern thought these are regarded largely as synonyms, but he had discovered that this was not true of the New Testament. He argued that there 'foregiveness' is the remission of sins, and does not extend, as in modern usage, to embrace the concept of 'restoration to fellowship with God'. In this narrower meaning of the word, God's forgiveness of sinful man is not dependent on the Death of Christ, since it is clearly affirmed in the Old Testament.

The examination of 'justification' in Paul convinced him that for Paul 'justification is not merely an equivalent for forgiveness'; 'it is a distinctive moment in the story of God's dealing with the soul of man'. He insisted that the New Testament and not our own Christian experience is the determinant of truth. Indeed 'the fact that we are not conscious of justification is irrelevant, provided that we perceive that justification is the gracious act of God which makes reconciliation ethically possible.' 'If we do not appreciate the necessity of this divine activity, our conception of reconciliation will be painfully inadequate; and we shall be unable to descry in the Atonement more than the revelation of divine love upon the stage of history.' The Atonement is achieved apart from our experience of it; yet it is incomplete if it remains unappropriated: 'Whatever that death has achieved stands outside ourselves until there is a believing response which makes the achievement a vital element in our approach to God.'

Dr. Taylor seeks also to make a clear distinction not only between 'forgiveness' and 'justification', but also between 'justification' and 'reconciliation', while fully appreciating the difficulty of so doing. He knows the question will be asked: 'How can we have a sense of remission of sins which stops short of fellowship with God; and can we know justification at all apart from its results in forgiveness and reconciliation?' But he nevertheless seeks to establish such a difference. It is here that many readers will feel uneasy. So long as it is the New Testament that is expounded Dr. Taylor will carry most readers with him; but in the area of contemporary speech and modern thought some will doubt if he is equally successful. Those who reject the need for any *objective* theory of the Atonement, will, of course, be unpersuaded by his arguments, and so also will those who feel that in modern speech it is quite impossible to restrict forgiveness to 'the remission of sins' and to exclude from it 'forgiveness of the sinner', including acceptance of him into happy, restored personal relationships. Others are so sure of the unchanging goodness of God that they will find it difficult to integrate into their thought any suggestion that God's attitude to men was changed even by the Death of Christ. This difference of opinion at this point is not surprising. The Church has continually declined to authorize as exclusively correct any one theory of the Atonement. No theory ever speaks equally to all men, and one may speak to the condition of any one generation better than another. It is no wonder therefore that Dr. Taylor's formulation fails to satisfy all. His books, however, do enable us to see with clarity what it is the New Testament writers believe about the Death of Christ and what was accomplished by it. They challenge us to make it our aim to do justice to these claims, even if we do feel that sometimes we have to translate their ideas as well as their Greek words, and sometimes even to 'demythologize' their vivid picture language.

Between 1920 and 1941 major publications had appeared at regular intervals. Then came a curiously long gap, 1941 to 1952, without any books from Dr. Taylor's hand. This was partly because the war years intervened, and Wesley College was commandeered for national purposes, and Dr. Taylor returned for some years to the circuit work of the Methodist church in St. Anne's. This change of situation made scholarly and literary work more difficult. There was, however, another reason. This was the fact that the next literary task he had set himself was one of unusual magnitude—a full scale commentary (based on the Greek text) on the Gospel according to St. Mark. When it finally appeared it contained more than 700 pages, and this number would have been much larger had not the commentary itself (apart from the introduction) been printed in small type in double columns on each page. This had been a massive undertaking. No care had been spared; nothing relevant to his theme had been left unconsulted; no point of view escaped undiscussed. Even in the most favourable circumstances a book of this kind, dealing exhaustively with every aspect of the subject, would have been the work of many years. It is no wonder that in view of the special difficulties of this period this book required ten years of concentrated work, to the exclusion of other major writings. When it was published it was quickly recognized that a commentary not only of unusual proportions, but also of quite unusual importance had arrived on the scene, and one that was likely to remain the standard work on St. Mark for a long time to come. Among his many important books it is perhaps this one which will ensure that his name will be remembered as long as biblical studies continue.

In this book also we find that happy blend, already noted, of a quick appreciation of new ideas, with the discernment which can distinguish the permanent from the ephemeral element in them. There is also a clear-sighted determination to refuse to reject the old and familiar merely because it is not new. So in relation to the Second Gospel he declared his continuing conviction that the traditional view which assigned it to John Mark was correct. 'Mark is not likely to have been named as the author unless there was very good reason to make that claim.' He defended too the tradition, first reported by Papias, that Mark had close links with Peter, who had been an actual eyewitness of some of the events recorded. He estimated the date of the writing of the Gospel as between A.D. 65 and 67, and favoured Rome as its provenance. The suggestion that the Gospel was first written in Aramaic before being translated into Greek he rejected, but insisted on the Aramaic quality of the Greek which necessitated an author with an Aramaic way of thinking. The presence of 'doublets' in the Gospel had led some to postulate a number of written sources from which the evangelist had derived his materials, but Dr. Taylor found the 'linguistic homogeneity' of the whole Gospel a strong argument against this. The only 'source' he regarded as 'proven' is what he called 'the Markan sayings collection'. The theory of a Proto-Mark, put forward to explain the occasional agreements of Matthew and Luke against Mark in its present form, did not convince him. He thought these unexpected agreements could be more probably explained as 'cases of textual assimilation'. On the other hand, his sympathetic appreciation of the new work of the Form-critics is shown by his careful analysis of the Gospel material into several groups: Pronouncement stores, Miracle stories, Stories about Jesus, Sayings, and Parables, with 'Markan constructions' and 'summary statements' listed separately.

The discussion of the Theology of the Gospel includes a long section on Christology, a foretaste of further studies to come later, and a recognition of 'affinities with Paul'. His discussion of the Historical Value of Mark is specially important, since this subject has in recent years loomed so large in biblical discussion. He fully concedes that 'Mark was not seeking to write history and is not a historian. His purpose was simpler. He wanted to tell how the Good News concerning Jesus Christ, God's Son, began.' He conceded also that 'apologetic, liturgical and catechetical motives guided Mark's undertaking.' He denied, however, that these interests had seriously distorted the Gospel, or so changed the material as to make it valueless for historical reconstruction. His experiments at Wesley College with the students had shown that, though narratives change in the telling, the nucleus of the story remains intact. Provided one is aware of non-historical motivation one can allow for it. He found the Gospel full of 'life-like touches' which give an impression of reality. He fully allowed that in themselves these were not a sure criterion of history. They could spring from the exercise of a vivid imagination. They nevertheless do present data on which a judgement may be based, especially if their character and distribution are considered'. When he begins to draw up a list of these impressive 'life-like touches', it goes on endlessly. By the time the end of chapter six is reached, 113 have been noted, and he is content to leave it there. Moreover he argues that the unpolished bluntness of some of the recorded events and the complete absence of embellishments at points where they might well have been expected, confirm the impression of objectivity. Events of this type include, for instance, the appointment of the Twelve (3:13), the Mission Charge (6:6), the Treachery of Judas (14:10), etc.

Besides insisting on the basic historicity of the units of the tradition, Dr. Taylor also asserts his belief in the historical value of 'the Markan outline'. He recognizes that many of the incidents occur in no ordered sequence, but he believes that Mark 'brings out the main points: the announcement of the Kingdom, the choice and appointment of the Twelve, the healing ministry, the conflict with the Pharisees, and the charges brought against Jesus'. His final conclusion is that 'here is a writing of first rate historical importance . . . Any attempt to tell the story of Jesus . . . must use, and is justified in using, the Markan outline.'

Into the discussion of historicity, Dr. Taylor introduced a frank consideration of the miraculous element in the Gospel. He did this out of a stern sense of obligation to readers who did not want to be fobbed off with ambiguous phrases. He knew, however, that this was a subject on which many people were very sensitive, and he shrank from hurting people unnecessarily. Personal letters at the time when he was writing this section show how difficult he found it to write: 'This section has caused me the greatest trouble', and, 'I am reassured that you think the section on miracles satisfactory.' The 'healing miracles' presented no real problem for him, but the 'nature miracles' did. Of these, he writes: 'It appears probable . . . that a miraculous interpretation has been superimposed upon the original tradition.' Legendary elements may have crept, for instance, into the accounts of the Baptism, the Transfiguration, and the Visit to the Tomb. The 'cursing of the fig tree' may have developed out of a parable. The stilling of the storm may have had a non-miraculous story as its origin. He felt also that the Christology of the nature miracles was different from that presented in the other parts of the Markan story, where the superhuman element in Jesus is hidden by His humanity, whereas in the nature miracles we see 'the God who throws off all disguise'. 'Are they coherent with the Incarnation?' he asks.

In the body of the commentary itself one finds an encyclopaedic discussion of every relevant issue, with note taken of every significant interpretation sponsored by other commentators. He brings an approach of great honesty to every problem. Though he strongly believes in the basic historicity of the materials, he frankly acknowledges items that must be designated 'embellishments', or even 'legends', by means of which a deep conviction is presented in a pictorial form. Of the voice that speaks to the disciples on the occasion of the Transfiguration he writes: 'A conviction gained by three intimate disciples is here expressed in direct speech.' Concerning the Rent Veil of the Temple at the time of the Crucifixion: 'An irresistible conviction of the new way opened between God and man here clothes itself in a legendary development of the tradition which is carried much further in Matthew.' He questions whether the extreme apocalyptic emphasis of Mark 13 represents the actual words and attitude of Jesus: 'All this is so different from Luke 17:22ff. that we are entitled to suspect the transposition of the original tradition into another key.'

This is a critical commentary of the highest quality, with no issue blurred or evaded, but it is also a commentary by an author who believed that in this Gospel he was dealing with material of supreme significance for our understanding of the purposes of God. After spending ten years in the closest possible relationship with this Gospel, he recorded his judgement that this is 'one of the greatest treasures of the Church, and one of the most influential and astounding books in the world'.

This detailed work on Mark served as a very valuable preparation for Dr. Taylor's next major publications. These were his important trilogy on the doctrine of Christ in the New Testament. The first two parts of this trilogy stand in close relation to his Markan studies. The first was called *The Names of Jesus* (Macmillan, 1953), and in it Dr. Taylor expounded and assessed the significance of the titles ascribed to Jesus, not only in the Gospels, but throughout the New Testament. He claimed that 'the names of Jesus are both the foreshadowing and the precipitate of Christology in its beginning; they anticipate developments and reveal what Christians thought in the creative period of theology. The question who Jesus is is approached best by considering how men name Him, for it is by His names that He is revealed and known.' About forty names are given separate consideration, some of which were in current use only for a short time and were then discarded as inadequate, but others proved themselves of enduring value and have continued to be used as a means of communicating the significance of Jesus. Even the term 'Messiah', which seemed so important when first used of Jesus, was one of those which soon fell into disuse. 'In the developments of terminology it is clear that the Messianic idea was the temporary mould in which the significance of Jesus was expressed.' Other 'moulds', therefore, had to be tried as a deeper appreciation of the significance of Jesus was developed. Indeed, he concluded, 'Christology is the despairing attempt of theologians to keep pace with the Church's apprehension of Christ.'

Next in sequence, and still more closely related to the Markan studies, was *The Life and Ministry of Jesus* (Macmillan, 1954). This was a supremely difficult task. Indeed it was a bold gesture of defiance against current trends. He himself called it a protest against 'too docile an acceptance of the more radical views of Form critics'. These views represented that the Gospels are to be understood as the vehicle of the early Christian faith about Christ, but the materials in them do not enable us to penetrate behind the subjective faith to the objective facts of history. In consequence scholar after scholar had announced that never again would anyone dare to write a Life of Christ. Indeed Dr. Taylor did not attempt precisely this, but he set himself to determine what elements in the Gospel narratives could without credulity be accepted as historical, and to arrange them in some kind of order, where the materials permitted it.

The study opens with an assessment of the earliest sources on which our present Gospels depend, and of the relative reliability of each of them. Mark is the earliest (unless 'Q' can claim this privilege) and in Dr. Taylor's judgement is 'a writing of first rate historical importance'. Even its outline of the main events he values as a 'useful and not misleading framework'. 'Q' and 'L' are also very valuable. In contrast the least reliable (historically) is Matthew's special source with its heightening of the miraculous element into fanciful proportions, as, for instance, in the episodes of the resurrection of the saints in Jerusalem after the crucifixion, and the descent of the angel at the Resurrection. It is these stories, writes Dr. Taylor, not without a touch of mischievous delight, which 'provide unbelief with its sharpest stones and Hollywood with its brightest inspirations'. They can confidently be discarded as unhistorical. It is recognized also that the Fourth Gospel is not primarily concerned with the presentation of history, but it nevertheless contains many items of historical worth. In any writer, whether ancient or modern, one has, of course, to expect some element of bias. History is told with different personal emphases. But 'the best way to deal with bias is to know that it is there and to ask what is its justification.' A historian need not despair because of it.

Soberly and realistically, therefore, he selects the units of the tradition which for him bear the stamp of historicity. Patiently he seeks to eliminate from them any elements that may reflect the writer's 'bias'. He arranges them in sequence, where arrangement is possible, and brings into being not only a portrait of Jesus, but a portrait in which historical development can be discerned. He knew that 'anyone who attempts to write a life of Christ is vulnerable at a hundred points', but he was convinced that this was a danger that had to be faced. Here, as elsewhere, Dr. Taylor did not lack courage to follow the line his judgement approved, even when it was out of the current fashion. It may well be, however, that, when the passing fashion has spent itself, and the mood to dismiss 'history' as irrecoverable and unimportant for faith has given way to whatever its successor will be, that Dr. Taylor's calm and dispassionate concern with 'what happened' will once again be recognized as a necessary ingredient of the true Christian Faith.

These two books were only the prelude to the final and most important book of the trilogy: *The Person of Christ in New Testament Teaching* (Macmillan, 1958)[1]. The author's modest hope was that it might make some contribution to an understanding of 'the greatest of all subjects, the meaning and significance of Christ'. This it undoubtedly has done.

His approach to the subject was original and eminently successful. It was a combination of two methods which have usually been regarded as alternative to each other rather than complementary. First he examined and analysed the Christological teaching of each book of the New Testament, without trying to determine the book's chronological relationship to other books, and recognizing that within any one book there

---

[1] This has recently been translated into French by J. Winandy and published as *La Personne du Christ dans le Nouveau Testament* (Cerf, Paris, 1969).

may be elements representing a period earlier than the date of the book itself. In this way the teaching was presented objectively and can be consulted objectively. In the second part of the book, however, he followed a chronological order, dealing with elements in all the books in the chronological sequence to which they appear to belong. Sometimes this involved decisions on date which others will dissent from, but it is a valid approach provided that opinions about date are not disguised as known facts. First in this second part came an assessment of 'the Divine Consciousness of Jesus', then the 'Christology of the Primitive Christian Community', followed in sequence by the special contributions of the major New Testament writers. The concluding chapters dealt with Christology in relation to the Trinity, to the idea of Kenosis and to Psychology, with a final chapter which looked 'Towards a Modern Christology'.

By a curious coincidence, almost at the same time, in 1957, Cullmann's book on *The Christology of the New Testament* was published in German, and in 1958 came an English Translation (S.C.M.). It is high praise for Dr. Taylor's book to say that it does not suffer at all in comparison, and, as he himself noted with satisfaction, both authors reached substantially the same conclusions at many important points, though the work of each scholar had been entirely independent of the other.

One topic may be mentioned in particular, since many writers have commented on its importance. This is Dr. Taylor's firm rehabilitation of a 'Kenotic' element in any adequate doctrine of the Incarnation. This is dealt with at length in Part II of the book in pages 260–276, but in Part I also a whole chapter is given to a detailed discussion of the Christological 'Hymn' in Philippians 2:6–11, with its famous phrase 'He emptied himself' (the Greek word for 'emptying' being *kenosis*). Dr. Taylor was inclined, with many other scholars, to regard this 'hymn' as pre-Pauline material, incorporated by Paul into his letter. But his inclusion of it stamps it with his approval. A generation earlier the so-called 'kenotic' type of Christology had been very persuasively presented by Mackintosh, and was then regarded almost as current orthodoxy. He had argued that if Christ is divine, and if nevertheless His life on earth was unequivocally human, then 'kenoticism in some form cannot be avoided'. Later writers, however, had rejected, almost disdainfully, this kenotic approach as wholly inadequate. Chief among these were W. Temple and D. M. Baillie. Temple, rather oddly it now seems, argued that if the 'Second Person of the Trinity' had been temporarily 'reduced' in an incarnation, the rest of the universe would have been 'in a dangerous state of instability' during that period. To this Dr. Taylor replied: 'Without presuming to define the manner of the divine operation one might suppose that the resources of the Trinity would be equal to the situation.'

Dr. Taylor states the point at issue thus: 'In His human life the Son of God is not omniscient and not omnipotent . . . If we have regard to these circumstances the opinion is surely justified that some form of kenosis-hypothesis is unavoidable.' His conclusion is: 'Christology is incurably kenotic . . . We cannot get rid of kenoticism. . . . The reason must be that self-limitation is an essential form of the divine manifestation. God is God when He stoops no less that when He reigns. He is a God who in revelation hides Himself.'

Dr. Taylor became outstanding as a scholar, but he never ceased to be a preacher. Even his most erudite books are apt to contain some reference to his conviction that good theology is 'preachable', and also passages which, for the urgency of their appeal, might have come from a sermon. For instance, the closing section of his book on the Person of Christ includes such sentences as these: 'We do not first discover who Christ is and then believe in Him; we believe in Him and then discover who He is . . . The natural man assumes that the secret of Christ's personality must be solved intellectually without self-committal to Him . . . The penalty of treating the Person of Christ as a purely intellectual problem is that He remains an enigma. The incognito is not interpreted. In addition to the study of the New Testament teaching a personal response to the revelation is necessary . . . Faith alone knows who Jesus is.'

In two of his books, however, he specifically puts his scholarship most effectively at the disposal of the preacher. They are *Doctrine and Evangelism* (1955) and *A Preacher's Commentary on the Epistle to the Romans* (1953), both published by the Epworth Press. Many preachers have proved the value of both.

His last published book, written from retirement in 1961, demonstrates his continued concern for students and their studies. At Leeds he had continually taught students who were required to offer Textual Criticism of the New Testament as a subject in degree examinations. He had often regretted the lack of a recent text book on the subject, of a kind he could confidently recommend to them. He now set himself to provide such a book in *The Text of the New Testament: A Short Introduction*. It achieves its purpose admirably. It is not meant for the advanced student who wishes to specialize in the subject, but as an introduction to the beginner. All discussion of new and speculative theories or abstruse details, which would not be appropriate in a 'short introduction', is therefore rigorously eliminated. With his characteristic orderliness he opens up the main aspects of the subject—Methods, Papyri, Uncials, Minuscules, Versions, Patristic quotations, Printed Editions, Textual Theories of Westcott and Hort and of Streeter, and developments since Streeter. Then follows a long section of particular value to the student, especially to one who has to prepare for examinations without tutorial guidance. It consists of a series of precise demonstrations of the technique of applying textual criticism to actual texts, whose wording is uncertain because of variant readings in the manuscripts. In each one the textural evidence is presented, interpreted and evaluated. Here we see a skilled teacher showing the student how to proceed.

This ends the tally of his books, and only the briefest mention can be made of two other areas of his scholarly work—his close association with the *Expository Times* and the many articles he wrote for learned journals. He was a frequent contributor to the *Expository Times* and his advice on authors and material was constantly sought by the editor. He never ceased to commend its value to students going out into the work of the ministry. It had enabled him as a young minister to keep in touch with the world of theological thought, and he coveted for others the same stimulation to their ministry that such a continuation of their studies could give.

Many of his articles both in the *Expository Times* and else-where made important contributions to scholarly discussion. It must suffice to mention only two, both dealing with the hypothetical document 'Q'. Dr. Taylor was persuaded of the basic validity of this hypothesis, and he continued to insist on the strength of the main arguments on which it was based, and provided new ones which gave it further support. He was sure that no other explanation of the close correspondences, in word and sequence of material, between Matthew and Luke in non-Markan sections dealt adequately with the facts of the case. Two important articles of his argued vigorously in its favour. The first one was 'The Order of Q' in the *Journal of Theological Studies*, new series, iv. 27–31, and this was later developed in another article on 'The Original Order of Q' published in the book *New Testament Essays in Memory of T. W. Manson* in 1959 (pp. 246–269). These articles demonstrated how the non-Markan material, reproduced in Matthew and Luke, can be shown to appear in a relatively similar order in each Gospel—a phenomenon unlikely to appear were the substance of 'Q' merely units of *oral* tradition. They did much to reinforce earlier conclusions about 'Q' in the face of attempts to represent it as an unnecessary and ill-founded speculation.

Another of his contributions to scholarship should perhaps also be mentioned in conclusion. As well as his own writing and lecturing, he was constantly providing inspiration and encouragement to younger men in whom he discerned some promise of scholarly achievement. It was his confidence in them, his unfailing readiness to offer his help in most generous measure, his determined insistence on their perseverance, and his own splendid example which enabled many of them to achieve far more than would have been possible without his prompting and his guidance. These remember him with special veneration and gratitude, but countless other students whom he taught and a still larger number whose minds were stimulated and enlightened by his writings, gratefully acknowledge the formative influence he has had upon their minds and their lives. And through his books that influence still continues.

I

Milestones in Books

THE BOOKS that have influenced me most in my thinking
are theological and expository, but I must not forget to mention
the debt I owe to the poets, to whom I was introduced by a
College friend. Among these was William Watson, the austere
beauty of whose poems made a deep impression upon my
mind. Greater was the influence of Browning and, in particular,
his *Ring and the Book*. Along with this poem I read *The Old
Yellow Book*, and I owe not a little to the depositions contained
in this volume for my abiding interest in source criticism. In
the Classics my imagination was captured by Vergil's *Aeneid*,
and I found as a boy how moving and attractive many of
Cicero's Epistles could be, especially, strange as it may sound
De Senectute.

About the age of seventeen the first serious theological book
which I read was James Denney's *The Death of Christ*, and I must
name this as my first milestone. I was fascinated by it, partly
by its style but more by its solid matter. What youth could
resist such a passage (on the Pastoral Epistles) as 'St. Paul was
inspired, but the writer of these epistles is sometimes only
orthodox'? It was to the Presbyterian Denney, and not to
Anglican theologians, that I owe my views regarding the
close connexion between the Eucharist and the doctrine of
the Atonement. 'The sacraments', Denney wrote, 'but especially
the sacrament of the Supper, are the stronghold of the New
Testament doctrine concerning the death of Christ.' In
the course of time I came to value other books of his, *Jesus
and the Gospel*, *The Christian Doctrine of Reconciliation*, and his
masterly commentary on *Romans* in *The Expositor's Greek
Testament*, but the most formative influence I received was
from *The Death of Christ*.

A second milestone was the reading of the works of William
Sanday of Oxford and the study of James Moffatt's *Introduction
to the Literature of the New Testament*. Sanday's *Outlines of the Life*

of Christ was to be a revelation of what method and critical insight could be. Later I read with avidity his *Life of Christ in Recent Research*, which introduced me to the works of Johannes Weiss, W. Wrede, and W. Bousset, and later his *Christologies Ancient and Modern*, but above all his great commentary on *Romans* in the *International Critical Commentary* series which, with so many more, has remained a lifelong companion. Along with these I must mention a pamphlet now almost forgotten, *Bishop Gore's Challenge to Criticism*, an essay which in temper and spirit is a model of the manner in which controversy should be conducted. I have always felt that it is a great loss to critical New Testament scholarship that no one has written a careful and detailed account of Sanday's work during the difficult period 1880–1920. We must be thankful, however, for Dr. A. Plummer's three valuable articles on 'William Sanday and his Work' in the *Expository Times* (xxxii. [1920–21]), which are full of interest and information. In a tribute to Sanday's memory in the *British Weekly* (Sept. 23, 1920) Dr. J. Vernon Bartlet compared the Oxford scholar with Westcott, Lightfoot, and Hort, and wrote:

> He had most in common with Hort, the most penetrating mind of the three, 'the scholar's scholar'. But he added to Hort's qualities of fine discrimination that lucidity of expression and literary style in which Lightfoot had the advantage over Hort. On the whole, however, it was Hort's temper of unresting inquiry, with a view ultimately to the big, abiding, fundamental theological issues, behind all biblical studies and all historical developments of Church doctrine and institutions, that appeared more and more plainly in him, marking the true affinity between the two scholars.

This discerning judgement from a nonconformist scholar adequately sums up the abiding impression which Sanday left upon many of us. I think I could identify an unnamed page of Sanday's writings at sight, but it is to his treatment of 'the big, abiding, fundamental theological issues' that I am indebted most of all. I met him only once, and I shall never forget his patient explanation of his well-known phrase 'a reduced Christology', by which he meant a Christology not in harmony with the Creeds.

My next milestone was B. H. Streeter's *The Four Gospels: A Study of Origins*. Undoubtedly this work was the outstanding contribution to the study of the Gospels in its period and, I think, is still of the greatest importance to literary and historical criticism. Its defence of the Proto-Luke hypothesis, to which I was first introduced by Streeter's suggestive article in *The Hibbert Journal* on the subject in October 1921, interested me profoundly, but no less influential was Streeter's stimulating presentation of Textual Criticism, especially the importance he found in the effect of the great Churches of Alexandria, Caesarea, Antioch, Cathage, and Rome upon the history of the text of the New Testament. Although I had gained much from the works of Westcott and Hort, Gregory, Kenyon, and Lake, it is to Streeter's contribution that I trace my abiding interest in this subject. I was also deeply indebted to his discussion of the Lucan Passion narrative which followed upon the contributions of A. M. Perry, J. C. Hawkins, and others, and is supplemented now by the works of W. Bussmann, J. Jeremias, and H. Schürmann, and I do not think that the criticisms which have been brought against this hypothesis are likely to prevail. It is natural that scholars rightly impressed by the immense value of the Markan narrative should hesitate to recognize the existence of other Passion narratives, but the future seems to me to lie with those who affirm that several of the great Churches, although dependent upon Mark, already had Passion narratives of their own, and that even Mark itself presupposes an earlier narrative. Streeter's Four Document hypothesis has been widely accepted, but is still in need of further discussion.

I place the next milestone in the slim volume of Dr. Martin Dibelius, *Die Formgeschichte des Evangeliums*, to which Dr. W. F. Howard drew my attention in 1928. This first edition was followed later by the revised and enlarged second edition, translated with the collaboration of the author by Professor B. F. Woolf in the well-known book, *From Tradition to Gospel*, in 1934, but although I learned much from the later volume, it is the first edition, despite its brevity, which influenced me most. It was bold, ingenious, and constructive. I think it was in this book that I first lighted upon the word *kerygma* now so popular, and it was from the reading of it that I came to realize the influence which the first preaching, described in the early chapters in the Acts and in 1 Corinthians 15 and other passages in the Epistles, must have exerted upon the formation of the Gospel tradition. 'In the beginning was the sermon' is the historic phrase with which E. Fascher described this emphasis in the work of Dibelius. I soon came to see that other factors besides preaching had to be taken into account—teaching, controversy, discussion, and worship—and, what is more important, that it was not enough to think of the earliest tradition as consisting of a mass of single fragments. From Dibelius and K. L. Schmidt I learned that the Passion narrative existed as a connected account from the first, since only by telling the story as a whole could the first Christians understand how it was that Jesus, who went about doing good, came to His tragic death upon the Cross. From Dibelius and Schmidt I moved on to Bultmann, Albertz, Bertram, Koelher, Easton, Grant, and the rest. New Testament research, it was obvious, was moving into a new field which gave promise of a deeper insight into the life and problems of the Christian community, and which raised the difficult, but fascinating, question of the influence which the community had upon the elucidation and the obscuring of the tradition. It was interesting and instructive to observe how easily the new wine intoxicated many students and led them to forget, or to ignore, the existence of eye-witnesses in the earliest decades and the conserving effects of teaching and worship. I found the distinction between *Paradigmen* ('models' or 'pronouncement-stories') and *Novellen* ('tales') illuminating, but the treatment of the sayings-tradition and of myths did not seem to me to add much to the ordinary principles of literary and historical criticism. While grateful for the new insights gained through Form-criticism, I did not lose my interest in source-criticism, and it seems to me that the comparative neglect of this discipline, which continues to the present day, is harmful to the best interests of Synoptic studies. How sad it is that we have to return once more to the defence of Q, M, and L, and even to rebut the delusion that the later evangelists used Matthew as a source!

It is not easy to find the next milestone in a single book. Several, in fact, contributed to a growing and permanent interest in New Testament theology. I gained not a little from

Bousset's *Kyrios Christos*, which unfortunately has never been translated, and from J. Weiss's *Das Urchristentum*, translated in *The History of Primitive Christianity* by four American scholars. The main interest of British scholars appeared to be the refutation of Bousset's claim that the use of the *Kyrios* title in primitive Christianity was due to pagan influences, but although this hypothesis was brilliantly refuted by A. E. J. Rawlinson and others, who found the 'Achilles' heel' in the currency of the cry '*Marana tha*' in Aramaic-speaking Christian worship, its decisive refutation tended to obscure the great emphasis which Bousset laid upon the worship of Christ as 'the Lord' in the first Hellenistic communities. Who could fail to be arrested by his forthright claim: 'The Jesus Paul knows is the pre-existent supramundane Christ, who was rich and became poor for our sakes, who was in the divine form and assumed the form of a servant, the Son of God whom the Father gave as an offering, the One who fulfils the prophecies and completes the promises'?

But other books besides Bousset's determined my interest in New Testament theology. In 1930 I had been much impressed by F. C. N. Hicks's *Fullness of Sacrifice*, and this interest was deepened by E. O. James's *Origins of Sacrifice: A Study in Comparative Religion*, which led me to study again G. Buchanan Gray's *Sacrifice in the Old Testament: Its Theory and Practice*, R. C. Moberly's *Atonement and Personality*, and J. McLeod Campbell's *Nature of the Atonement*. No doubt the detailed picture which Bishop Hicks gave of an ancient Hebrew offering was composite, but it seemed to me to throw much light upon the Passion sayings of Jesus and the doctrine of the Atonement. More formative, however, in their influence were Joachim Jeremias's *Die Abendmahlsworte Jesu* [1935], (Eng. Tr. *The Eucharistic Words of Jesus* [1955]), Rudolf Otto's *Reich Gottes und Menschensohn* [1933], (Eng. Tr. *The Kingdom of God and the Son of Man* [1938]). To these I must add, as regards Christology, H. R. Mackintosh's *Doctrine of the Person of Jesus Christ* and P. T. Forsyth's *The Person and Place of Jesus Christ*.

Many other works have broadened my studies, but as milestones those I have mentioned stand out, and I am grateful for the opportunity to mention them and also to commend them to others. (*1959*)

II

The Creative Element in the Thought of Jesus[1]

IS THERE a creative element in the thought of Jesus, and, if so, in what form does it gain expression? I prefer to put the question in this form rather than to speak of His originality, for in this word there is a tone of condescension, as if one classified Him with other great leaders of mankind. Having said this I agree that it will not be possible to avoid the word without artificiality, but at any rate, in speaking of 'the creative element', I have made my intention clear.

From many notable discussions of Primitive Christianity we gain the impression that His thought was not creative. He was not a philosopher and certainly not a scientific theologian, but a teacher and a prophet, and, of course, it is assumed, teachers borrow and prophets are declarative. It is the ubiquitous community that is creative by reason of its endowment with that dubious entity 'the collective mind', and it is brilliantly creative, evolving *ex nihilo*, or from next to nothing, moving ideas and doctrines which have deeply affected the course of Christian thought and history. Or again, St. Paul, that shining example of Hellenistic thought, is the real founder of Christianity, who, nevertheless, turns out on examination to be much more Jewish, and indeed Rabbinical, than we had supposed, as Professor W. D. Davies has recently shown in his *St. Paul and Rabbinic Judaism*. As a prophet, it is held, Jesus was receptive and absorbent. Almost everything He ever said can be found in the Mishnah or the Talmuds, mixed, it is true, with much else of which the less said the better. The original element in His teaching is to be found in His speech

[1] An Address given at the Commemoration Day service at Handsworth College, Birmingham, 5th November, 1948.

36

forms, His sparkling epigrams, His poetic genius; but not in certain ideas which stand in an organic relationship to New Testament theology and the later developments of Irenaeus, Origen, and Athanasius. Between Jesus and Paul yawns a gap.

Two initial considerations should lead us to pause before we give our assent to this view.

First, we must recognize that the greatest Old Testament prophets were creative in their thinking. Amos rose above the idea of a national god to the magnificent conception of Yahweh as the God of the whole earth, who brought the Philistines from Caphtor and the Syrians from Kir (Amos 9:7). Jeremiah broke through conventional assumptions and discovered afresh the values of personal religion. Above all, that genius of the Exile, whose name we do not know, but of whom we speak as Deutero-Isaiah, bequeathed to the world the immortal portrait of a Suffering Servant, about whose identity scholars have speculated in a prolonged and unfinished discussion admirably described in Professor C. R. North's invaluable *Suffering Servant in Deutero-Isaiah.* Prophets, it would appear, can be as creative as Bach and Shakespeare; they are not corybantic gospellers or conventional ethical preachers. On the contrary, they may sting a generation into new ways of thinking and inspire peoples yet unborn.

Secondly, we must face the inherent probability that a rich and persistent movement like Christianity began with a creative personality. This likelihood is at its strongest when the greatest of His followers speak of Him with veneration and awe. It is of no lay figure that St. Paul writes: 'Who, being the form of God, counted it not a thing to be clutched at, to be an equality with God', or that the author of the Epistle to the Hebrews describes as 'the radiance of God's glory' and 'the express image of His essence'. Nor can St. John have been thinking of an ordinary person when sonorously he writes: 'And the Word became flesh, and tabernacled among us, and we beheld his glory, glory as of the only begotten from the Father, full of grace and truth.' These writers impress us as men lifted out of themselves into a new world of thought and action. Doubtless, they used a new idiom and were themselves creative thinkers, with an originality which Christianity has always stimulated in converts, whether African lawyers, medieval monks, or Bedford tinkers; but they would be the first to reject the suggestion of being innovators, and to confess their insolvency apart from the initial impulse received in Christ. In their own estimation, they are the 'unprofitable servants' of an incomparable Master.

The question must naturally arise: How comes it that the creative character of the thought of Jesus has been so widely ignored and denied? Two suggestions may be offered in reply.

First, we have failed to assimilate the immense extensions of our knowledge of religious thought and practice in the centuries preceding and following the beginning of the Christian era. We have not seen facts in their true perspective. Consider, for example, our greatly increased knowledge of comparative religion. Max Müller's *Sacred Books of the East*, and innumerable monographs on special themes, have familiarized us with the complexity and wealth of religious ideas the world over. Against this background how small appears the work of an obscure prophet in the petty tetrarchy of Galilee! The idea of 'the dying god' finds worldwide illustration. What is distinctive in the story of the Cross? Again, with many gaps, we have greatly enlarged our knowledge of the Mystery Religions, and where knowledge has failed imagination has exercised her potent spell. The enthusiast has read with awe the mystic words: 'I have eaten out of the *tympanon*, I have drunk out of the *kymbalon*, I have become an initiate of Attis.' In imagination he has accepted the invitation of Chaeremon to dine at the table of the Lord Serapis on the fifteenth at nine o'clock, and, in consequence, has found it easy to suppose that the Christian Eucharist owes more to the age than it owes to Jesus. Then, we have greatly extended our knowledge of mystical religion. The Hermetic writings and the sacred books of Mandaism tell of divine saviours who dwell among men and wing their way to the realms of light. Dazzled by discoveries, the investigator has passed lightly over the dates of relevant documents. W. Bauer rewrote his commentary on the Fourth Gospel in order to insert impressive quotations from the Mandaean writings, despite the fact that the earliest, the Book of John, is not earlier than the seventh century A.D. H. Delafosse maintained that the Gospel is the Christianized version of a Gnostic writing. Thus, in the first decades of this century the Fourth Gospel fell into the background as a source for the life and teaching of Jesus, and there it remains until we accept the astringent supplied by the opinion of F. C. Burkitt that it is useless to go to Mandaism as 'a key to unlock the mysteries of early Christian development', and learn from M. Goguel that the Gospel contains valuable material which the historian may not ignore. The Synoptics are shaken for us by Form Criticism. From Bultmann we learn to think of 'community-sayings' and from Bertram discover that the Passion Story is a collection of cult-narratives, and it is with surprise that we find this same Bultmann, helped by the anodyne of Barthian theology, writing a vigorous sketch of the thought of Jesus, and at some cost that we discover that the liturgical *motif* is often a conservative influence.

It goes without saying that, if used with critical discernment, many of these discussions provide us with an equipment which earlier students did not possess. Unfortunately, they are often taken at their face value. As examples of this I cite Loisy's *Birth of Christianity* and Bishop E. W. Barnes's *Rise of Christianity*, in which opinions about theology and Christian documents are expressed with a confidence which makes the New Testament expert shudder. From such books it is easy to infer that, apart from its ethics, Christianity is outmoded, and that, while we still look to its Founder with wistful admiration, He is not a creative personality comparable with Charles Darwin or Karl Marx. Even the high priest of Barthianism, Karl Barth himself, has described the Rabbi of Nazareth as 'one whose activity is so easily a little commonplace alongside more than one other founder of a religion and even alongside many later representatives of His own "religion" '.

The second suggestion I have to offer comes nearer home. The modern theological student is blessed by the aid of monumental encyclopedias, commentaries, and monographs. I mention in particular the invaluable works of Hastings, Cheyne and Black, Charles, Billerbeck, and Kittel. We are right to devote days and nights to the spoiling and appropriation of these treasures, but there is one peril against which we must be on our guard if we are in any true sense to appreciate the originality of Jesus. When we have painfully traced the background and antecedents of His teaching, it by no means

follows that we are really acquainted with His mind and
thought. All we have gained is material on which a judgement
can be based, prolegomena, warnings against bypaths, the
constructive gains of innumerable failures. We have still to ask
how Jesus used older and contemporary ideas, how He combined them and made them a whole. Genius borrows, but it
also transmutes; it leaves nothing as it finds it, but prints
upon all an original stamp. It is precisely in this matter that
much contemporary research is wanting. It is sometimes
assumed that, if we know all there is to know about the history
of the idea of the Son of Man, of the Messiah, and the Suffering
Servant, we know what Jesus thought. In fact we know
nothing of the kind. Schweitzers are always needed to tell us
that Jesus is the great Unknown, a stranger to our generation
and its ways of thinking, and yet is the most modern of all
because in His hands are the keys of life and of death.

In what follows I shall try to show the justice of this claim,
as I treat such themes as Messiahship, the Son of Man, the
Suffering Servant, the Cross, the Resurrection, and the
Parousia, and the creative use which Jesus made of these
ideas.

(1) I begin with the attitude of Jesus to Messiahship. This is
no new question, although often it has prematurely been
regarded as settled. Did not Jesus say expressly to the challenge
of Caiaphas 'I am'?

The problem arises from the manifest reserve of Jesus and
the injunctions to secrecy which He laid upon the healed and
upon His disciples. 'Hold thy peace,' He cried to the demoniac
in the synagogue at Capernaum who declared that He had
come to destroy them, and hailed Him as 'the Holy One of
God'. 'See that thou say nothing to any man,' He said to the
leper. 'Do not even enter the village,' He commanded the
blind man near Bethsaida. Mark says that He suffered not the
daemons to speak because they knew Him, and relates that
both at Caesarea Philippi and at the descent from the mount of
Transfiguration He charged His disciples to tell no man of
Him. It may be that we have made too much of His reply to
Caiaphas, for Matthew, supported by Luke, says that He
replied 'Thou hast said,' and important MSS. attest the same

words in Mark. The reply was not negative; it probably meant 'Yes, but I shouldn't put it quite like that.'

For upwards of fifty years British scholarship has been preoccupied in refuting the thesis of Wrede that the charges to secrecy are a literary device on the part of Mark to explain why Jesus was not confessed as the Messiah until after the Resurrection. And the answers are sound. It has pointed to the confession of Peter, the entry into Jerusalem, and the inscription on the Cross, and has argued that the first preachers would not have embarrassed themselves by proclaiming a crucified Messiah unless Jesus had been condemned as such. But a refutation is never a complete answer. It is necessary to account for the facts in a more credible way. And, in the main, we have paid Jesus the doubtful compliment of a policy of expediency: He did not want to provoke a popular uprising! This explanation is sound, but it is not the whole truth. I suggest that Messiahship as He understood it was not a title, nor primarily an office, but fundamentally a destiny. Messiahship was what He would do by dying and rising again. It was for this reason that He could not accept an honorific title which on the lips of others meant something entirely different. As one who healed the sick and cast out daemons He was the Messiah already, but a hidden Messiah, because His redemptive Messianic task remained to be fulfilled. He was *Messias absconditus* and *Messias futurus*.

Here I would point out how creative this thought was; it determined His conception of Himself and His estimate of His purpose. It is reflected in His sayings, but it lies deeper than any of them. So far from being compelled to part with His saying about the taking away of the Bridegroom, we must recognize that the rape of the Bridegroom is of the essence of His mission as He saw it and believed it to be.

(2) I turn next to the vexed question of the Son of Man. On this question no generally agreed solution has been reached. We have ransacked the sources, we have studied the Psalms, Ezekiel, Daniel, the *Book of Enoch*, and Ezra 4, we have examined the concept of Primal Man; we have sifted the Rabbinical writings and have analysed Mark, Q, M, and L, but the problem still baffles us. In part our difficulties are due to the

complexity of our sources, but still more, I think, to our slowness to admit that Jesus may have made an original use of the idea.

It is not easy to decide what use we are to make of the *Book of Enoch*. Dr. J. Y. Campbell thinks the Similitudes are 'quite inadequate to prove anything'. Our younger scholars are more optimistic. The Norwegian Nils Messel holds that the Son of Man in *Enoch* is a collective symbol, a view which reminds us of T. W. Manson's interpretation, while William Manson, J. Bowman, and M. Black are disposed to think that in some circles of pre-Christian Judaism the concept was interpreted Messianically. Few who have read T. W. Manson's *Teaching of Jesus* can be insensible to the fascination of the view that the Son of Man is the Elect Community, the Suffering and Saving Remnant, wholly devoted to God. Hitherto, many scholars have hesitated to accept his suggestion because in *Enoch* the Son of Man seems so clearly to be a superhuman personality and because it is difficult to give a collective interpretation to many of the sayings of Jesus. Manson, however, does not deny that 'Son of Man' is also a personal designation, and he provides for this interpretation by saying that, when the disciples fail to rise to the demands of the ideal, Jesus 'stands alone, embodying in his own person the perfect human response to the regal claims of God'. In his *Historic Ministry of Jesus* the late Dr. C. J. Cadoux made a very effective use of this conception, and it is made easier of acceptance by the idea of 'corporate personality' expounded by Dr. H. Wheeler Robinson and Dr. A. R. Johnson.[1]

It may be that, if we are to make further progress, we may have to make a bolder use of conjecture. Nothing but good can result from the use of constructive imagination, provided we control it by fidelity to all the available facts and provided it is subjected to full and frank discussion. I suggest that in the Gospels the collective interpretation is overshadowed because, at the time when they were composed, the personal and eschatological aspects of the idea were dominant. It is possible that, influenced by Daniel 7, there was an earlier stage in which the collective use of the term 'Son of Man' was more prominent in the thought of Jesus. Now that we identify so

[1] *The One and the Many in the Israelite Conception of God* (1942).

closely the 'Kingdom of God' with the 'Rule of God', we require a conception which includes the idea of the domain in which the Rule is exercised, and the idea of the Elect Community supplies this want. Moreover, it is significant, I think, that to the end a communal aura surrounds the idea that the Son of Man 'must suffer', illustrated in the sayings about cross-bearing and drinking the cup and in the association of Peter, James, and John, with Jesus in Gethsemane. We also gain a more vivid and intelligent understanding of the Mission of the Twelve, when the disciples went forth two by two to announce the imminence of the Rule of God, if at that time Jesus expected its correlative, the setting-up of the Elect Community. Greatly daring, I suggest that we have not yet finished with the saying: 'Ye shall not have gone through the cities of Israel, till the Son of man be come' (Matthew 10:23), and that, in our haste to allow for the fact that Matthew has applied the saying to the circumstances of the ninth decade, we may be destroying evidence. I can understand Matthew's procedure in adapting an embarrassing saying no longer relevant to the circumstances of his day, but not the invention of such an utterance to further the missionary expansion of the Church. If the saying is genuine, Schweitzer made a valuable contribution to the problem of Gospel Origins when he made the failure of the Mission of the Twelve a turning point in the Story of Jesus. If this suggestion is conjectural, it is certain that Jesus made a creative use of the Son of Man conception when He rebaptized it in terms of the Suffering Servant of Isaiah 53, and to this question I now turn.

(3) In his *Jesus the Messiah* William Manson has suggested that in the *Similitudes of Enoch* the Son of Man, the Messiah, and the Servant are identified; and, with varieties of emphasis, this identification is accepted by W. D. Davies and M. Black. The most impressive passage is *Enoch* 48:4:

> He shall be a staff to the righteous whereon to stay
>   themselves and not fall,
> And he shall be the light of the Gentiles,
> And the hope of those who are troubled of heart.

Here, undoubtedly, it is pertinent to recall the Servant passages in Isaiah 42:7, 50:4 and 61:1f. But what we still miss in this proposed identification is the idea of the *Suffering* Servant, the doctrine that 'the Son of Man *must suffer*' and give his life '*a ransom for many*'; and, so far as we know, this is an original element in the thought of Jesus, the clearest sign of His creative thinking. Even if it could be proved that He was preceded in this interpretation, His originality would remain; for it is no condition of genius that it must not borrow. Otherwise, the creativeness of Homer, Shakespeare, and Bach would have to be reconsidered. What genius does is to make new thoughts current coin; and, on this principle, there can be no manner of doubt to whose teaching the doctrine of a Suffering Messiah is due. The only known precursor is Deutero-Isaiah, and with the Ethiopian eunuch research still cries: 'I pray thee, of whom speaketh the prophet this? of himself, or of some other?' It was Jesus who first dared to believe that the ideal of the Servant was embodied in Himself, and combined it with the Messianic hopes of His countrymen. It was He who first taught that the Son of Man must suffer. How little the Christian community can be credited with this creative doctrine is seen in the fact that in the New Testament there is a progressive diminution of interest in this doctrine, to the subsequent impoverishment of post-Apostolic Christianity.

(4) We come now to the question whether Jesus had a doctrine of the Cross. I believe that He had, provided we do not delimit too sharply the word 'doctrine'. Of course, we shall not want to represent Him as an Irenaeus or an Athanasius, still less an Anselm or an Aquinas. Ratiocinative thought is not to be looked for in the poet of the Beatitudes. But is it decently credible that a creative thinker, who perceived that the Son of Man 'must suffer', and believed that He Himself was that Son of Man, had no sort of idea why He must suffer, or what blessings His sufferings would confer upon men? Had He no answer, save that such was the Father's will? If, with Hastings Rashdall, we explain the 'ransom-saying' as meaning that 'His death, like His life, was a piece of service or self-sacrifice for His followers, such as they themselves might very well make for one another', we shall have to admit that His thought was commonplace rather than original. And if, further, we explain

away His words about 'the blood of the covenant' and 'the cup' that He must drink, and if we transform the cry of desolation, 'My God, my God, how is it that thou hast forsaken me?' into a paean of pious confidence in God, we shall have to limit ourselves to the view that He died to reveal the love of God, a truth which, so far as we know, He never even mentioned. But if, on the contrary, we see Him steeped in the ideas of the Old Testament, and take seriously His words about 'blood', 'the covenant', and 'the cup', we shall have reason to believe that He thought in terms of sacrifice. To Him the sacrificial principle was as familiar as evolution is to ourselves, and it is reasonable to suppose that He used this idea creatively.

The Gospels show that He sat loose to ritual practices and had little use for the sacrificial system as such, although He did command the leper to make the prescribed offering and bade men offer their gifts after they had been reconciled one to another. But equally clearly His sayings show that He rejected the scirbal interpretation of the Law, but, none the less reinterpreted it with amazing insight. Why should He not have done the same with the idea of sacrifice? In Judaism a sacrifice is a gift to God and a means of communion with Him: it can be degraded to the offering of a bribe; it can be elevated to the idea of a communal offering in which the worshipper shares. It is in this realm of ideas that we have most reason to think that the thought of Jesus moved. The place of a material oblation is taken by the offering of Himself, and a crude substitution is obviated by the vital connexion between Himself and the Beloved Community and its faith-relationship to Himself. It is true that later faith was interpreted more personally and more mystically by St. Paul and St. John, but in His teaching it is implicit in actions, the effective actions of eating and drinking. Thus, at the Last Supper He interprets the Bread as His Body and the Wine as His blood poured out for many, and commands that they are to be eaten and drunk as such; and in this way the faith-relationship is more objectively conceived. All these ideas are fundamentally Jewish; there is no reason to seek the key for them in pagan feasts or mystery-conceptions.

We may go further. His words about drinking the cup show

that He was conscious of feeling the weight of that wrath of God which rests upon human sin; not as a penalty transferred from the guilty to the guiltless, but as the destiny of a love which makes itself one with sinners and shares their plight. St. Paul did no more than transform this thought into an epigram when he spoke of Christ as 'made to be sin on our behalf, that we might become the righteousness of God in him' (2 Corinthians 5:21). The cry of desolation reveals that redemptive suffering broke His heart.

In all this construction there is nothing extraneous or anachronistic. We are far indeed from the classroom or Origen or the cloisters of St. Thomas. Its advantages are that, without artifice or strain, we can keep close to His recorded sayings and His Jewish heritage of thought; we can do justice to His originality and thereby establish a genetic relationship between His thought and later Pauline and Johannine developments, not to speak of Christian theology in general.

(5) I turn next to the place of the Resurrection in the thought of Jesus. If He spoke of death, He did not think of it as disaster. Faithful to Old Testament thought, He believed in the victory of divine purpose. Thus, whenever He says that the Son of Man will be rejected and killed, He adds 'and after three days rise again'. By this expression He meant, in accordance with the idiom of Hosea 6:2, the shortest interval of time. He believed that He would go before them into Galilee; that is, they would find Him there already. And find Him they did. Whatever may be said of the Empty Tomb, His disciples knew that He had appeared to them, and that He was 'known of them in the breaking of bread'.

(6) Lastly, it is in the same context of thought that we may place the prophecy of His Parousia. For reasons which are intelligible His sayings on the future Coming of the Son of Man are obscured by the garish foliage of Christian hope. But the parting of the leaves does not reveal nothing. Much of His eschatology was 'realized eschatology', but not to the exclusion of a doctrine of the End Time, any more than for St. Paul Justification by faith, itself a piece of realized eschatology, precluded belief in the Last Judgement. Doubtless,

with that foreshortening of history which is characteristic of prophetic speech, He left the impression that His return would be speedy. Doubtless also He has already come in His Spirit in the life of the Church and the crises of history. None the less it is in harmony with His teaching that He should still come in the consummation of history to reveal Himself to His own. And though we do not know when or how, we still look for a New Age 'wherein dwelleth righteousness' and for the Parousia of Him who 'makes all things new'.

I conclude that, for the reasons that I have given, the thought of Jesus was creative, controlling, determining.

Christianity is an unfolding, not a recast; it is true to type, not cross-bred. It has been able to receive and absorb into itself elements from other religions and philosophies, but always on the condition that they be born again and baptized into the name of Christ. And it has been able to do this because it begins with the dynamic creative personality of Him in whom God breaks into our world of space and time.

Professor E. F. Scott has aptly compared Christianity with a river and its tributaries; but the better similes are those used by Loisy at the time when he argued against himself in *L'Évangile et l'Église*. Christianity is like a reverberating echo which becomes more sonorous the farther it travels. It is like a tree the essence of which appears as truly in its branches and leaves as in the germ from which it springs; it is this because it is rooted in the Living Christ of God.

(*1948*)

III

The New Testament Origins of Holy Communion

MANY ATTEMPTS have been made to trace the origins of the Christian Eucharist to the influence of the Mystery Religions and of Hellenistic religious ideas in general. The Mystery Religions centred in the worship of gods and goddesses associated with oriental religions, Cybele, Osiris, Isis, Attis, Mithras, and other divinities, and gained a wide following in Greece and Rome in the centuries immediately preceding and subsequent to the spread of Christianity. Secret rites and initiation ceremonies in communities of men and women of different races, which promised deliverance from fate and death, made a wide appeal to those who no longer found satisfaction in the ancient religions of Greece and Rome; and it is not surprising that many scholars have looked for the origin of the Christian sacraments in the sacred rites and religious meals of these communities. These speculations have been shown to be false and misleading.[1] There are few references to sacred meals in the texts which describe the Mystery Religions, and, whatever may be true of later times, the late date of the evidence makes it improbable that they were operative in the formation of the Gospel tradition in the period A.D. 30–60. Moreover, the religious ideas embodied in the teaching of Jesus Himself and of St. Paul can be far more credibly traced to the Old Testament, to sacrificial meals, and to the religious associations of the practices of eating and drinking among the Hebrew people, to the Servant ideas of Isaiah 53, the Covenant

[1] See H. A. A. Kennedy, *St. Paul and the Mystery Religions*, pp. 256f., C. Clemen, *Primitive Christianity and its Non-Jewish Sources*, pp. 257–66, T. Wilson, *St. Paul and Paganism*, p. 183, N. P. Williams, *Essays Catholic and Critical*, p. 389, A. E. J. Rawlinson, *The New Testament Doctrine of the Christ*, pp. 270–84, M. Goguel, *The Life of Jesus*, p. 187, C. Gore, *The Reconstruction of Belief*, pp. 724f.

conception, and the expectation of the great Messianic Feast connected with the eschatological expectation of the coming of the kingdom of God. 'Blessed', said the man who sat at table with Jesus, 'is he who shall eat bread in the kingdom of God' (Luke 14:15).

Whether the basic idea of sacrifice in the Old Testament is that of a *gift* or that of *communion* with God is a disputed question. Probably we have to allow for both conceptions. In the case of Jesus we may infer that it was not so much the Temple sacrifices as the sublimated idea of sacrifice in the figure of the Suffering Servant of the Lord (Isaiah 53) which deeply influenced His thought.[1] As the Servant was to give his soul 'an offering for sin' (*asham*),[2] so He had come to give Himself 'a ransom for many'.[3] At the giving of the Covenant on Sinai sacrifice was offered, and Moses said, 'Behold the blood of the covenant, which the Lord has made with you concerning all these words', and of the people it was said, 'They beheld God, and did eat and drink.'[4]

Although the idea of the Covenant does not often appear in the sayings of Jesus, it is mentioned twice at the Last Supper—indirectly in Luke 22:29f., 'And I appoint (covenant) unto you a kingdom, even as my Father appointed (covenanted) unto me, that you may eat and drink at my table in my kingdom,' and explicitly in Mark 14:24, 'This is my blood of the covenant.' The great Messianic Feast[5] appears to be in mind in the passage from St. Luke just quoted, and probably also it is implicit in the stories of Feeding in Mark 6:35–44 and 8:1–9, which were fellowship-meals anticipating the future inauguration of the Kingdom. From time immemorial the common meal has been invested with religious significance in the ancient east, and this is probably the reason why eating and drinking with tax-gatherers and sinners (Mark 2:16) on the part of Jesus gave such grave offence to the scribes. All these ideas lie behind the action of Jesus when on the last night of His earthly life He broke bread and gave wine to His disciples in the Upper Room at Jerusalem. Passover ideas also must have filled His mind.

---

[1] Cf. Mark 8:31, 9:31, 10:33f., 45; 14:24; Luke 22:37.   [2] Isaiah 53:10.
[3] Mark 10:45.   [4] Exodus 24:11.   [5] Isaiah 25:6.

On the day before the Last Supper Jesus sent two of His disciples, identified by St. Luke as Peter and John, into the city to make preparations for the Passover meal.[1] By an arrangement apparently made in advance they were to look for the unusual sign of a man carrying a jar of water. Following him, they gave the message of Jesus to the householder, 'Where is my guest room, where I may eat the passover with my disciples?', and being shown 'a large upper room furnished and ready', they prepared the Passover meal.

According to St. Mark's account the Last Supper was the Passover meal, and very many scholars accept this view. Others, however, influenced by John 18:28, which says that the priests did not enter the Roman praetorium, that they might not be defiled, but might eat the Passover, and by John 19:14, 'Now it was the Preparation of the passover', as well as by indications within St. Mark's Gospel, maintain that the Supper was celebrated twenty-four hours earlier. This is probably the better view, but learned opinion is almost equally divided.[2] In any case Passover ideas must have been in the minds of Jesus and His disciples. They must have remembered ancient Jewish tradition,[3] according to which on the eve of the departure from Egypt the Israelites killed and roasted a lamb 'without blemish', and ate it with unleavened bread and bitter herbs. When their children asked the meaning of the custom, they were to say: 'It is the sacrifice of the Lord's passover, who passed over the houses of the children of Israel in Egypt, when he smote the Egyptians.'[4] The Passover, then, was a feast of remembrance; it powerfully called to mind a great act of deliverance. These traditions will have been recalled during the course of the Last Supper, and the Fourth Gospel rightly interprets the significance of Jesus when the Baptist addresses Him with the words: 'Behold, the Lamb of God, who takes away the sin of the world.'[5] It is against this background of Old Testament teaching that we can best understand the New Testament narratives of the institution of the Christian Eucharist.

[1] Mark 14:12–16; Luke 22:7–13.

[2] See J. Jeremias, *The Eucharistic Words of Jesus*, pp. 14–60, A. J. B. Higgins, *The Lord's Supper in the New Testament*, pp. 13–23, Vincent Taylor, *The Gospel According to St. Mark*, Appendix K, pp. 664–7.

[3] Exodus 12.   [4] Exodus 12:26f.   [5] John 1:29, 36.

I

The New Testament narratives of the institution of the Eucharist are three, and perhaps four, in number: Mark 14:22–5, 1 Corinthians 11:23–5, Luke 22:14–19a, and possibly the fragment Luke 22:19b–20. Of these, the narrative of Mark 14:22–5 was already old at the time when the Gospel of St. Mark was written,[1] and it may be older and more original than St. Paul's account in 1 Corinthians 11:23–5. Luke 22:14–19a is also old, and apart from 19a is independent of St. Mark's account. Whether we should add Luke 22:19b–20 depends on how we interpret the thorny textual problem presented by these verses, which are omitted by Codex D, the Old Latin manuscripts *a d ff*[2] *i l*, and by *b* and *e* and the Old Syriac version which place 19a before 17.

The antiquity of the Gospel narratives is shown by the Aramaic constructions they contain, and that of St. Paul's account by the fact that he expressly says that he is delivering to the Corinthians that which he had 'received of the Lord', a phrase by which we are to understand, not a story received by direct revelation, but one handed down in liturgical tradition, probably that of Antioch in Syria. According to Joachim Jeremias,[2] St. Mark's short narrative contains no less than twenty Semitisms and Palestinian idioms.[3] He concludes that it is the nearest to the Aramaic account of the Lord's Supper. St. Mark's wording, he says, is 'earlier than the development and enlargement of the Aramaic original of the Last Supper, which took place long before A.D. 49–50, the results of which are to be found in Paul'.[4] He even attempts to define a pre-Markan form of the tradition, which omitted the phrase 'my blood of the covenant', a phrase which is impossible in Aramaic, where a noun with a pronominal suffix cannot govern a genitive, and must have been added in the first decade after the death of Jesus.[5] In a footnote he explains that the possibility that the word 'covenant' (which appears also in 1 Corinthians 11:25) represents Jesus' own idea is not denied. 'On the contrary', he writes, 'it is highly probable that Jesus declared that the time for the New Covenant had come, particularly

[1] A.D. 65–7.   [2] In *The Eucharistic Words of Jesus*.   [3] Ibid. pp. 118–27.
[4] Ibid. p. 132.   [5] Ibid. p. 135.

because the promise of Jeremiah 31:31ff. was highly popular in his days, as is seen from the writing of the community of the new covenant at Damascus.'[1]

The Markan narrative is preceded by the account of the meal when Jesus was eating with the Twelve during which He foretold His impending betrayal.[2] To the question, 'Is it I?', asked by one after another, He gave the enigmatic reply: 'It is one of the Twelve, one who is dipping bread in the same dish with me.' That He was thinking all the time of His impending death is clear from His words: 'For the Son of Man goes, as it is written of him, but alas for that man by whom the Son of Man is betrayed! It would have been better for that man if he had not been born.' Then follows the account of the institution of the Eucharist, the text of which is as follows:

> And as they were eating, he took bread, and when he had blessed, he brake it, and gave to them, and said, Take ye: this is my body. And he took a cup, and when he had given thanks, he gave to them: and they all drank of it. And he said unto them, This is my blood of the covenant, which is shed for many. Verily I say unto you, I will no more drink of the fruit of the vine, until that day when I drink it new in the kingdom of God (Mark 14:22-5).

St. Matthew's version[3] is an edited form of St. Mark's narrative in which he adds the word 'eat' after 'take', the command, 'Drink you all of it', the phrase 'for the forgiveness of sins' after 'for many', and 'my Father's kingdom' instead of 'the kingdom of God'.

The blessing is an act of thanksgiving, and according to Jewish custom would take the form: 'Praised be Thou, O Lord our God, King of the Universe, who dost bring forth bread from the earth.' 'Take' manifestly refers to the broken bread which they are to receive as bearing a new significance. The word 'is' does not describe a relationship of identity and would not be expressed in Aramaic. 'On the whole, the least unsatisfactory translation is Moffatt's "Take this, it means my body", because it suggests a certain valuation which Jesus

[1] Ibid. p. 135 note.   [2] Mark 14:17-21.   [3] Matthew 26:26-9.

has given to the bread both by His words and by His prophetic action in breaking it.'[1] Just as the Old Testament prophets[2] gave expression to their message by the aid of dramatic action, and thereby sought to make it effective, so Jesus meant the broken bread to be a means whereby His disciples might share in the power of His self-offering and the virtue of His approaching death. In like manner the wine is given a sacrificial significance in the words: 'This is my blood.' The saying expresses the idea that 'as of old dedicated blood was applied in blessing to the people of Israel,[3] so now His life, surrendered to God and accepted by Him, is offered to, and made available for men.'[4] The phrase 'of the covenant', whether original or added, expresses this idea, and it is further conveyed by the words 'which is shed for many'. These words show that Jesus had reflected long on Isaiah 53:12, which reads: 'Because his soul was delivered up to death, and he was reckoned among the transgressors, and he bore the sins of many.' There can be no doubt that the words of institution strongly affirm the atoning significance of Christ's death, and for this reason the Eucharist stands at the centre of Christian worship. 'For many' does not mean 'many, but not all', but in accordance with Hebrew idiom 'many in relation to the one sacrifice'. Jeremias rightly says that it has an inclusive meaning, 'the sum total, consisting of many', and he explains that 'shed' has a future reference, since in Hebrew and Aramaic the present participle is used, not only for the actual present, but also for the immediate future. Thus, he translates the whole phrase by the words: 'which is going to be shed for the whole world'.[5]

The third saying in the account, 'Verily I say unto you, I will no more drink of the fruit of the vine, until that day when I drink it new in the kingdom of God', shows that eschatological hopes were in the mind of Jesus at the Last Supper. He was thinking of the final consummation of all things. This idea is found also in the narratives of St. Paul and St. Luke and belongs to the essential meaning of the Eucharist. 'The drinking

[1] Cf. Vincent Taylor, *The Gospel According to St. Mark*, p. 544.
[2] Cf. Isaiah 20:2, Jeremiah 19:10; 28:10, Ezekiel 4:3, 1 Kings 22:11. Cf. also Acts 21:11, and see R. Otto, *The Kingdom of God and the Son of Man*, pp. 299–305.
[3] Exodus 24:8.
[4] Vincent Taylor, *Jesus and His Sacrifice*, p. 138.
[5] *The Eucharistic Words of Jesus*, p.151.

of the cup is a present participation in that fellowship (of the consummated kingdom) so far as it can exist here and now.'[1]

The one saying we miss in the narrative is 'This do in remembrance of me', which is found in 1 Corinthians 11:24f. and Luke 22:19b. The saying is regarded by many critics as a Christian formation which expresses in direct speech a conviction of which Christians were conscious; but it may well be a genuine saying which St. Mark's liturgical narrative took for granted. P. Benoit[2] explains it as a rubric and says: '*On ne récite pas une rubrique, on l'exécute*', 'One does not quote a rubric; one carries it out.' Jeremias[3] suggests an interpretation which is worthy of note. He points out that of four examples of the phrase translated 'unto remembrance' in the Greek Old Testament,[4] three speak of God's remembrance, and that in Scripture when God 'remembers' somebody He acts. 'He does something, He sits in judgement and grants His grace, He fulfils His promise.' Jeremias therefore renders the saying, 'Do this that God may remember me', and relates it to the Parousia. The community beseeches God to remember His Messiah by bringing the consummation to pass.[5]

II

The second narrative of institution is 1 Corinthians 11:23-5:

> For I received of the Lord that which also I delivered unto you, how that the Lord Jesus in the night in which he was betrayed took bread; and when he had given thanks, he brake it, and said, This is my body, which is for you: this do in remembrance of me. In like manner also the cup, after supper, saying, This cup is the new covenant in my blood: this do, as oft as ye drink it, in remembrance of me.

To this account St. Paul immediately adds: 'For as often as ye eat this bread, and drink the cup, ye proclaim the Lord's death till he come.'

---

[1] Vincent Taylor, *The Gospel According to St. Mark*, p. 547.
[2] *Revue Biblique*, xiviii (1939), p. 386 note 2.
[3] *The Eucharistic Words of Jesus*, pp. 159–65.
[4] Leviticus 24:7, Psalm 37 (38), title, 69 (70), title, Wisdom 16:6.
[5] *The Eucharistic Words of Jesus*, p. 164.

It is not surprising that some scholars have assigned priority to this account in view of the early date of the Epistle.[1] In any case, the account is very old, older than the Epistle itself, for it is a tradition which the Apostle had received and handed on to the Corinthians. But it is less marked by Semitisms than St. Mark's narrative and the difference shows signs of interpretation. Thus, St. Paul adds to the words 'This is my body' the explanatory phrase 'which is for you', to which later scribes added the participles 'broken' or 'given'. Further, the words 'This cup is the new covenant in my blood' appear to be a modification of an earlier reference to the wine designed to exclude the possible misunderstanding on the part of Gentile Christians of the term 'blood'. In St. Paul's account the covenant is established 'in' or 'by' Christ's blood; in St. Mark's narrative the wine signifies His blood 'shed for many'. St. Paul does not include this allusion to Isaiah 53:12, although probably the Servant idea is implied in his reference to the night when Jesus was 'delivered up'. Essentially, however, the basic assumptions of the two narratives are the same. The sacrificial nature of Christ's atoning death is common to both, also the idea that to receive the bread and the wine is to share in its power. That this is St. Paul's belief is clear from his words in 1 Corinthians 10:16, 'The cup of blessing which we bless, is not a participation in the blood of Christ? The bread which we break, is not a participation in the body of Christ?' The acts of eating and drinking 'proclaim the Lord's death', and the eschatological aspect of the rite, although more fully expressed in the sayings of Jesus quoted by St. Mark and St. Luke, is clearly emphasized in St. Paul's words 'until he come'.

The command to continue the celebration of the Supper is expressed twice.[2] The command 'Do this' means 'Perform this act', not 'Sacrifice this'.[3] This mistranslation is not only impossible linguistically, but it is unnecessary exegetically, since sacrificial ideas are already present in the use of the terms 'blood' and 'covenant'. The teaching of St. Paul elsewhere shows that he viewed the Last Supper in this light. In 1

---

[1] A.D. 51.   [2] 1 Corinthians 11:24, 25.
[3] Cf. Robertson and Plummer, *The First Epistle of St. Paul to the Corinthians*, pp. 245f.

Corinthians 5:7 he writes, 'For our passover also has been sacrificed, even Christ', and in Romans 3:25 he speaks of the act of God in setting forth Christ to be a means of atonement, through faith, by His blood.[1] The 'covenant' is described as 'new' or 'fresh'. Jeremiah 31:31 is certainly in the Apostle's mind, but he has no thought of excluding the ideas and associations of the covenant at Sinai described in Exodus 24:1–11. He clearly conceives of the bread and wine as 'supernatural food', as the warnings of 1 Corinthians 10:1–13 testify, where he says that our fathers 'all ate of the same spiritual food, and all drank of the same spiritual drink'; but it is alien to his teaching to suppose that he thinks of the elements as changed in substance. They are 'spiritual' or 'supernatural' in view of the meaning which Christ gives to them. The kind of communion which the Apostle describes is closely related to his teaching concerning union with Christ, but it is union with Him in the power of His reconciling death.

III

The third narrative of institution, Luke 22:14–20, is composite and may include two or even three different versions of the incident. The text is as follows:

14. And when the hour was come, he sat down, and the apostles with him. 15. And he said unto them, With desire I have desired to eat this passover with you before I suffer: 16. for I say unto you, I will not eat it, until it be fulfilled in the kingdom of God. 17. And he received a cup, and when he had given thanks, he said, Take this, and divide it among yourselves: 18. for I say unto you, I will not drink from henceforth of the fruit of the vine, until the kingdom of God shall come. 19a. And he took bread, and when he had given thanks, he brake it, and gave to them, saying, This is my body (19b. which is given for you: this do in remembrance of me. 20. And the cup in like manner after supper, saying, This cup is the new covenant in my blood, even that which is poured out for you).

[1] See my commentary on *Romans*, pp. 32f.

It has been widely maintained that St. Luke derived verses 14–18 from his special source, L. If this view is correct, these verses may be the account current in certain circles in Palestine, presumably at Cæsarea. The source may have included 19a, 'And he took bread, and when he had given thanks, he brake it, and gave to them, saying, This is my body', but it is more probable that this passage, which agrees closely with Mark 14:22, was appended by the Evangelist in the process of compiling the Third Gospel. Verses 19b–20, to which reference has already been made, are enclosed in double brackets by Westcott and Hort,[1] and are regarded by them and by many other scholars as a later interpolation.[2] But in recent years there has been a growing tendency on the part of many scholars to accept the passage as genuine.[3] It is contended that, although 19b–20 has much in common with Mark 14:24 and 1 Corinthians 11:24, there are important differences, and that their style is not Lukan.[4] It is maintained that 19–20 belongs to a third variation of the liturgical form of the narrative of the institution of the Eucharist.[5] These matters are still the subject of learned debate. Naturally the discussion has turned upon the question of the authenticity of 19b–20. It is possible, however, that whether this passage belongs to

[1] Cf. 'Notes on Select Readings', pp. 63f. in *The New Testament in the Original Greek*.

[2] The arguments are (a) the probability that 19b–20 is a later addition intended to restore the order Bread-Cup in the Lukan narrative, and (b) the suspicious coincidence of its words with 1 Corinthians 11:24f.

[3] Jeremias, *The Eucharistic Words of Jesus*, p. 106 note 1, gives a list to which may be added M. Goguel, F. Kenyon, S. C. E. Legg, A. J. B. Higgins, and C. S. C. Williams. It is argued (a) in order to obtain the order Bread-Cup it would have been more natural to omit the first reference to the Cup in verse 17; (b) that the textual evidence for the passage, which includes all Greek MSS. except D, all the versions except the Old Syriac, Marcion, Justin Martyr, and perhaps Tatian, is very strong, and (c) that the passage may have been omitted in order to preserve the account of the Eucharist as an *arcanum*, a secret to be hidden from profane eyes, 19a being preserved as a cue for instructed Christians much as the first line of a poem may stand for the whole. Cf. Jeremias, *op. cit.*, p. 105. For 19a, cf. G. D. Kilpatrick, *The Journal of Theological Studies*, XLVII (1946), p. 53.

[4] The Greek phrase in Luke 22:20 rendered 'even that which is poured out for you' refers to 'in my blood' and would be more correctly expressed in the dative case. Cf. Jeremias, *op. cit.*, p. 102.

[5] Cf. Jeremias, *op. cit.*, p. 103, A. J. B. Higgins, *The Lord's Supper in the New Testament*, p. 44.

the original text of Luke or not, it is derived from a primitive source and is thus a different account of the story.

One point of the greatest interest and importance is the difference of doctrinal emphasis in 14–18 as compared with 19–20. The former is exclusively eschatological; the latter, as in St. Mark and St. Paul, connects the Eucharist with the atoning death of Christ. It is quite unnecessary to set the one account against the other, since both ideas are attested by the narratives of St. Mark and St. Paul. The objection that there is no textual support for the separate existence of 14–18 is not serious,[1] if the Evangelist derived these verses from the L source and himself added either 19a or 19–20.

If 14–18 is the narrative of a Palestinian community, one must infer that this community centred its interest, perhaps exclusively, in the joyful anticipation of the consummation of the kingdom of God. There is no good reason why it should not have been so, for we cannot assume that every Christian community celebrated the Eucharist in precisely the same form from the beginning. The references to 'the breaking of bread' in Acts 2:42, 46, 20:7, 11 may suggest that also in the primitive Jerusalem community attention was concentrated upon the joyful experience of the Risen Christ and the expectation of His speedy return. If this inference is justified, concentration upon the eschatological aspect of the Supper was a stage which passed into a larger unity, and if we are right in tracing the addition of 19a to the hand of St. Luke, we can see this stage in process of transition. A parallel example of eucharistic teaching may perhaps be seen in 1 Corinthians 11, for there St. Paul appears to be emphasizing the importance of the death of Christ to a degree which apparently the Corinthian Christians had not sufficiently recognized. It is not a case, however, of earlier and later developments in the tradition itself, for both ideas, the eschatological and the soteriological, are plainly present in the ancient Markan and Pauline narratives, and both go back to Jesus Himself. Parallel to the eschatological hope, and not to the exclusion of it, primitive tradition preserved the belief that Jesus interpreted the Supper as a memorial of His death and as a sharing in the power of

---

[1] Cf. Jeremias, *op. cit.*, p. 104, A. J. B. Higgins, *op. cit.*, p. 40.

His Sacrifice. Throughout the centuries, and still today, the Church celebrates the Eucharist in its twofold aspect of a present experience of fellowship with the Living Christ and a joyful anticipation of the perfected kingdom. We 'proclaim the Lord's death until he comes'. In doing this, we do not observe a rite of Hellenistic origin, but fulfil the intention of Christ, who instituted the Eucharist to give to those who love Him a part in His redeeming love, the experience of His presence here and now, and the opportunity to plead that His Sacrifice be fulfilled in a renewed and transformed world. As Charles Wesley sang:

> *This eucharistic feast*
> *Our every want supplies;*
> *And still we by His death are blessed,*
> *And share His sacrifice.*

(*1959*)

IV

The Origin of the Markan Passion-sayings

I

MY FIRST WORDS must be words of thanks for the great
honour done to me in appointing me President of this Society*
for the year 1954–5 in succession to Professor Rudolf Bultmann.
I also wish to express my deep regret that circumstances
beyond my control prevent me from being present at Marburg
to deliver the address in person.

Since the President's address is not followed by discussion
it would be inappropriate for me to treat the subject I have
announced in a controversial manner and with a view to the
sustaining of a particular thesis. In some respects this custom
is burdensome; but it has at least this advantage that a speaker
may choose a great theme of current interest, and, without
attempting to disguise his own opinions, may draw attention
to the issues which are involved and to considerations which
need to be weighed and pondered by all in a common desire
to reach positive results.

Of the importance of the origin of the sayings in Mark
8:31; 9:12, 31; 10:33f., 45; and 14:24 there can be no question.
It must obviously make a great difference to our understanding
of the teaching of Jesus, and of His person, whether we regard
these sayings as genuine utterances of His or whether we find
their origin in the work of the Christian community. The
view that the sayings are *vaticinia ex eventu* is widely held, but
no less so the belief that they are original utterances of Jesus.
It would, I think, be a tragedy if differences of opinion upon
this question were regarded as signs of intellectual standing, as
marking the distinction between learned and enlightened
conclusions and the obscurantism of more conservative views.
The universally esteemed article of Joachim Jeremias on
Παῖς Θεοῦ in the fifth volume of Kittel's *Theologisches Wörterbuch
zum Neuen Testament* has made such a distinction ridiculous;

* The Society for New Testament Studies.

and in the better intellectual climate which this article has established it seems appropriate to reconsider the wider issues that are involved. To attempt to discuss the arguments on both sides in a purely detached and unbiased manner would, I think, be an artificial undertaking, since personal preferences would undoubtedly colour the presentation of the case. It seems better to indicate certain matters which need to be reviewed by protagonists and then to describe, since the speaker inclines to the less radical alternative, the hesitations which conservative scholars feel about the hypothesis that the sayings are *vaticinia ex eventu* and the particular arguments on which they prefer to rely. It is in the persuasion that nothing but good can come from scholars who are prepared to explain themselves one to another that this address is delivered.

In what follows I shall not discuss in detail a third view which theoretically at least is possible, the view that the Passion-sayings, while shaped by the believing community, may none the less express ideas which Jesus Himself held. As a mediating position this view is open to attack on both sides, and all that is important in it can be considered in connexion with the stronger alternatives. In varying degrees all views have to find room for the work of the community, for even among those who accept the sayings as genuine many would agree that the sayings, especially Mark 10:33f., have not been preserved in all cases in the form in which they were originally spoken. The inevitable effects of transmission, first from Aramaic to Greek, and then from one speaker to another in the primitive communities in Palestine and the Hellenistic world, are such that verbatim preservation is not to be expected although naturally there will be varied opinions as to the extent to which modification has taken place. The real issue is whether the phrase, *vaticinia ex eventu*, is a valid characterization of the sayings in question.

In considering this issue it is, I think, a mistake of method to begin with the sayings themselves. We ought rather to begin with the New Testament Epistles and the Acts of the Apostles, and to consider what place the idea of the Suffering Servant had in the thought and teaching of the first Christian communities. We ought to begin at the end and work backwards.

II

It is a fact of importance that in the later New Testament writings, the Johannine, the Pastoral, and remaining Catholic Epistles, the idea of the Suffering Servant, as applied to Jesus, is either entirely absent or appears, as for example in I Timothy 2:6, 'Christ Jesus, who gave himself a ransom for all', as a traditional formulation modelled apparently on Mark 10:45. Hebrews 9:28, 'Christ, once for all offered to bear the sins of many', the only 'Servant-passage' in the Epistle, seems also to be a form taken over from Primitive Christianity. The origin of the ideas implicit in John 1:29, 'Behold, the Lamb of God which taketh away the sin of the world', is disputed, being variously attributed to the lamb of Isaiah 53:7, the Passover lamb, the lamb slain at the morning and evening sacrifice, and the horned lamb of the Apocalypse. If the influence of Isaiah 53 is recognized, the very limited extent to which the prophecy is reflected in the Fourth Gospel is still strikingly illustrated. I Peter 2:22–4, 'Who did no sin, neither was guile found in his mouth . . . who his own self bore our sins in his body upon the tree . . .', is capable of different interpretations, being either a traditional idea taken over by the writer or more probably an independent use of the teaching of Isaiah 53 which is woven into the argument of the Epistle. If the non-Petrine authorship and late date of the Epistle are affirmed, this creative use of the Servant conception is exceptional in the later New Testament writings; and to this extent, it may be contended, its teaching is more in line with Petrine authorship and the earlier date assigned to I Peter by E. G. Selwyn and others. In sum, we may say that during the second half of the first century A.D. the Servant idea in the New Testament is in eclipse. The passages which make use of it in interpreting the work of Christ are in the main dependent upon the doctrinal tradition of an earlier generation.

The two passages in which Matthew definitely cites the Servant poems of Deutero-Isaiah illustrate this decline. Matthew 8:17 and 12:18–21 are probably quotations from an earlier collection of testimonia, and it may be significant that neither is a Passion-saying; the former illustrates the healing activity of Jesus by the words, 'Himself took our infirmities and bore our diseases' (Isaiah 53:4), the latter His charge to maintain silence regarding His healings and exorcisms by the language of Isaiah 42:1–4 which describes the Servant's humility and compassion. As we shall see, both Matthew and Luke, despite changes, reproduce the Passion-sayings of Mark in an abbreviated form. One cannot speak of a creative use of Isaiah 53 during this period.

A similar conclusion is suggested by the Pauline Epistles. The few passages which imply the use of the Servant conception have been taken over by the Apostle from primitive Christian usage. Among those which have been explained in this way are I Corinthians 11:24; 15:3; Romans 4:25; 8:32, 34, and Philippians 2:6–11. If we look carefully at these passages, we find that the debt to Isaiah 53 is small and in some cases doubtful. It may be that the phrase 'according to the scriptures' in I Corinthians 15:3f. implies a reference to Isaiah 53, but this view is not certain and in any case other Old Testament passages are in mind. I Corinthians 11:24, 'This is my body, which is for you', is at best a very general allusion to the Servant conception, and I Corinthians 11:25, in its reference to Christ's blood, lacks the Markan phrase 'which is poured out for many'. Romans 8:32, 'but delivered him up for us all', may echo Isaiah 53:12 (LXX), 'his soul was delivered up unto death', but Romans 8:34, apart from its distinctive allusion to Christ's intercession, contains only the significant Pauline phrase 'for us', which in parallel forms, 'for you', 'for our sins', 'for us all', has a much broader foundation in Old Testament sacrificial ideas and reflects primitive Christian beliefs. Romans 4:25, 'who was delivered up for our trespasses', may be, as Professor Bultmann has suggested,[1] 'a traditional formulation' quoted by the Apostle; and it is in favour of this explanation that we can then explain the words which follow, 'and raised for our justification', as a Pauline amplification of the saying designed to give expression to the belief that Christ died and rose again because of our trespasses and our justification, an exposition defended by modern commentators. Paul develops, that is to say, a primitive liturgical phrase as a musician uses a traditional motif. It is widely believed that Philippians 2:6–11 is steeped in Servant teaching, and much

[1] *The Theology of the New Testament*, 1, 31, 46, 82.

support has been given to Professor Lietzmann's contention that the passage is a 'pre-Pauline hymn'.[1] The balanced phrases, and to some extent the vocabulary suggest that the 'hymn' is earlier than the Epistle, composed either by Paul himself or some unknown predecessor. The lexical argument does not seem to me to exclude the former alternative, but in either case we are probably dealing with a poem already composed at the time when Paul wrote to the Philippians.

All the indications in the Pauline Epistles, it may be claimed, go to show that the Servant teaching as applied to Christ is pre-Pauline; and, coupled with the evidence of the later New Testament writings, they suggest that by the time Paul wrote this teaching was already on the wane. It is significant that Paul, like John and the writer of Hebrews, never applies the name 'the Servant' to Jesus. I have suggested elsewhere[2] that the explanation may be that, while Paul rejoiced to think of himself as 'the slave', *ebed*, δοῦλος, of Christ, he may have shrunk from applying the name to Christ, with a consequent loss to his theology. This suggestion is highly speculative and may not be necessary. The truth may be that in the period when he wrote, the name was no longer a current Christological title, but was subsumed within the Christian meaning of the name 'Son of Man' or 'the Man from heaven'. It may by significant that, although the Servant conception continues to be applied to Christ in I Clement 16:3–14 and Barnabas 5:2, the name 'the Servant' is not used, although it appears in the Didache 9:3. Apart from I Peter 2:22–4, where the name also is wanting, it would appear that from the fifties onwards, and perhaps from a still earlier time, the teaching was a traditional survival. The title is among the names that passed because other names were felt to be more adequate and meaningful.

The question arises how the evidence of the Acts fits into this situation. Does it confirm, or refute, the contention that in the second generation of early Christianity the doctrine of the Suffering Servant as applied to Christ, if not obsolescent, was in the background of Christian thought? The answer, I suggest, is that the evidence strikingly confirms this view.

[1] Cf. R. Bultmann, *op. cit.* 1, 27, 125, etc.
[2] *The Atonement in New Testament Teaching*, p. 66.

As is well known, the name 'the Servant' is applied to Jesus in Acts 3:13, 'the God of our fathers has glorified his Servant Jesus'; 3:26, 'God, having raised up his Servant'; 4:27, 'thy holy Servant Jesus'; and 4:30, 'through the name of thy holy Servant Jesus'; and the idea that Jesus is the Servant is found in the story of the Ethiopian Eunuch in Acts 8:26–40. There is nothing in the Acts to suggest that this teaching is that of the author, and is therefore to be dated A.D. 80 to 90, when this writing was compiled. Rather it belongs to his primitive Aramaic sources and has survived from the earliest days. In a scholarly article by Professor H. J. Cadbury on 'The Titles of Jesus in the Acts' in *The Beginnings of Christianity*, v, pp. 354–75, it has been suggested that it is doubtful if the term 'Servant' in Acts 3:13, 26; 4:27, 30 is reminiscent of Isaiah 53, but is suggestive of the language in which notable figures of sacred history, Abraham, Jacob, Moses, Job, Daniel, and Zerubbabel, are described.[1] This explanation is not convincing in view of the references to 'delivering up' (3:13), 'raising' (3:26), and 'glorifying' (3:13), which echo the language of Isaiah 53. There is more to be said for the view of Professor Oscar Cullmann, who points out that of the four passages in the Acts, two stand in Petrine speeches and two in a prayer spoken in unison when Peter is present, and who says, 'It is probably not too bold to conclude from this fact that the author preserves the clear memory that it was the apostle Peter who by preference designated Jesus as the "Suffering Servant of God".'[2] This suggestion is in harmony with the story of the Confession of Peter (cf. Mark 8:32) and with the use of the Servant conception in I Peter 2:22–4, directly if the Epistle is Petrine, indirectly if it is assigned to Peter by an anonymous author.

The contention, supported by the evidence as a whole, that the Servant Christology was at its height, not during the

---

[1] Cf. also R. Bultmann, *The Theology of the New Testament*, 1, 50.

[2] Professor Cullmann also writes: 'The Christology of the apostle Peter, if we may dare to use this expression, was quite probably dominated by the concept of the *ebed Yahweh*.' He also affirms that the narrative concerning the Ethiopian eunuch is 'the chief evidence that Jesus was explicitly identified with this *ebed Yahweh* in the first century, and that the vivid memory was clearly preserved that Jesus himself so understood his divine mission'. Cf. *Peter, Disciple, Apostle Martyr*, Eng. Trans., p. 66f. Cf. also Acts 13:47.

sixties, the seventies, and the eighties, but in the period A.D. 30–50, and in the earlier of the two decades more than in the later, deserves the most serious consideration. This Christology remained as a primitive Christian deposit, thrusting its way to the surface in later times like rocks on the surface of the soil which tell of deeper strata, but in this period it is not a dominant and characteristic layer; it no longer determines the colour and the substance of Christian thinking. Already in the Pauline Epistles, the Epistle to the Hebrews, and the Johannine writings it is overlaid by the Logos Christology. Changing the figure, we may say that, after the earliest period of Apostolic Christianity, the Servant Christology is the echo of a distant voice which reverberates from time to time in the later decades. It is against this theological background, I suggest, that the origin of the Markan Passion-sayings must be considered.

III

With Mark 8:31; 9:12, 31; 10:33f., 45, and 14:24, the passages in question, Mark 1:11; 2:20; 9:7, and Luke 17:25; 22:37 may conveniently be associated. It is widely agreed that these sayings reflect the influence of Isaiah 53, although as regards some of them this view has been questioned. If this influence is admitted, the question under debate becomes a burning issue.

It is necessary to examine the passages more closely. The words of the divine voice at the Baptism and Transfiguration, 'my Beloved Son' (Mark 1:11; 9:7), recall Psalm 2:7 and Isaiah 42:4, and possibly also Genesis 22:2, Isaiah 44:2, and 42:4. If, as seems probable, the idea of the Messianic Son is combined in these words with that of the Servant of the Lord, the question arises whether this combination of ideas carries with it that also of the *Suffering* Servant, and on this matter commentators disagree. Mark 2:20, 'The days will come when the bridegroom shall be taken away from them', recalls Isaiah 53:8, 'By oppression and judgement he was taken away', and appears to have this prophecy in mind. The debt of Mark 8:31; 9:12, 31; 10:33f., 45 to Isaiah 53 seems clear in the references to suffering, rejection, death, and exaltation, and by the use of the phrase 'for many' in Mark 10:45, as again in

Mark 14:24 where Christ's 'blood of the covenant' (Exodus 24:8) is said to be 'poured out for many' (Isaiah 53:12). Luke 17:25 is of like tenor, and Luke 22:37 specifically quotes Isaiah 53:12. This is the only saying in which Isaiah 53 is directly quoted, the rest of the passages being allusive, as if a conviction gained otherwise than by a simple process of borrowing were being expressed in the familiar language of Scripture. Luke 22:37 also has distinctiveness if καὶ γὰρ τὸ περὶ ἐμοῦ τέλος ἔχει may be translated, with E. Klostermann[1] and others,[2] 'For my life draws to its end.' In these sayings we have a solid body of teaching in which the suffering, rejection, death, and victory of Jesus are illuminated by Deutero-Isaiah's description of the Suffering Servant of the Lord. It is probable that Mark 10:33f., in its detailed references to mocking, spitting, and scourging, has been conformed to the Markan story of the Passion, and it may be that the explicit phrase 'the third day', here and in Mark 8:31 and 9:31, has replaced a more general allusion to resurrection. These matters will be variously estimated. The major problem is whether the sayings are genuine in substance or whether they are *vaticinia ex eventu*; and to this question I now turn.

IV

Instead of debating the arguments *pro* and *con* I propose to examine the bearings of the theological situation already described on the origin of the Markan Passion-sayings. Several points of importance arise.

(1) First, I suggest the whole question of 'community-sayings' calls for reconsideration. This issue, however, is much too large and much too controversial to be raised in the present address. I therefore confine my observations to the *vaticinia ex eventu* hypothesis as it appears in the light of Servant Christology in the New Testament.

(2) I suggest that, if the doctrine of the Suffering Servant was no longer a living issue at the time, A.D. 60–90, when the Gospels were written, we shall need to look again at the view that Mark introduced this teaching into his Gospel on theologi-

---

[1] *Das Lukasevangelium*[2], p. 214.
[2] H. B. Swete, *Studies in the Teaching of our Lord*, p. 111.

cal grounds. It becomes more difficult to maintain that the Evangelist sought to contrast the divine plan of salvation, that the Christ must suffer, with the human conceptions of the disciples because his readers needed instruction about the necessity of the suffering of Jesus. And it is harder to maintain that the prophecies of suffering were shaped under the influence of the confessions and the *kerygma* of the community.[1] The theological situation would not, of course, exclude the possibility that the Servant teaching in the Gospel of Mark is a kind of doctrinal archaism, since, as we have seen, traditional forms of this teaching lived on in the later New Testament writings. Such a view, however, would be a very attenuated form of the *vaticinia ex eventu* hypothesis, hardly to be contemplated without misgivings by its advocates. Or it might prove necessary to take second thoughts about the presence of the Servant teaching in the Passion-sayings, and to argue that, as *vaticinia ex eventu*, they are influenced not by this teaching, but rather by the more general sacrificial ideas which are implicit in the Pauline formula, 'Christ died for us.' But, in this case, the difficulty would arise whether, after all, we really can exclude the idea of the Suffering Servant from the Gospel sayings. It would seem that the theological approach I have outlined increases the difficulty of maintaining that the Passion-sayings are to be traced to Mark and to the doctrinal needs of the believing community.

(3) Thirdly, in the light of what has been said, the brilliance and originality of the Servant teaching as applied to Christ's sufferings derives a new importance. So distinctive is this teaching that it used to be maintained, and is still generally held, that the combination of ideas is not pre-Christian. Today it is claimed that, in certain circles, Isaiah 53 was interpreted Messianically even in pre-Christian times.[2] If this view is accepted, it does not necessarily detract from its Christian form, for in this form a vital point is added, namely the conviction, not only that the Servant is the Messiah, but that

[1] Cf. E. Percy, *Die Botschaft Jesu*, p. 240.

[2] Cf. the article mentioned above by J. Jeremias; also W. Manson, *Jesus the Messiah*, pp. 98–101, 171–4; W. D. Davies, *Paul and Rabbinic Judaism*, p. 279f; J. Bowman, *The Expository Times*, LIX, 287f.; M. Black, *The Expository Times*, LX, 14f.; and especially by H. Hegermann, *Jesaja 53 in Hexapla, Targum und Peschitta* (1954).

the Servant-Messiah is Jesus.[1] This interpretation is likely to have been the product of prolonged reflection based upon the Scriptures and the life of Jesus, and its origin is to be found in the profound insight of an individual rather than in the depths of the consciousness of the community. It is at this point that the importance of the time element appears. Where in primitive Christianity are we to find such an interpreter? Not, apparently, in Paul, the writer of Hebrews, and the Fourth Evangelist, since for them the interpretation was already traditional. Peter is suggested by Professor Cullmann, but it is notable that he feels compelled to say that 'Jesus himself so understood his divine mission.'[2] Whether this is so, is one of the alternative views under consideration, and all that is claimed at the moment is that any other suggestion is difficult in consequence of the very early currency of the teaching.

(4) Fourthly, in view of the theological situation, the claim that the Passion-sayings are authentic calls for reconsideration, and, in particular, whether its implications, as regards the nature of the Gospel tradition and its historical aspects, put this view out of question. This issue is so important that I propose to devote the final section of my address to it, giving special attention to the problems which the affirmative answer raises.

v

(1) Some of the arguments would secure wide assent, as, for example, the submission that, if the prophecies are genuine, a strong link is established between the teaching of Jesus and the beliefs of the Jerusalem community. Speculative explanations are no longer necessary. The teaching was current because it was remembered. This submission has the advantage of simplicity, but it is of limited value so long as the major problem remains.

(2) Much the same may be said of the suggestion that the decay of the Servant Christology in the New Testament is easily explained if the teaching of Jesus about His suffering and

[1] Cf. T. W. Manson, *The Servant-Messiah.*
[2] *Op. cit.* p. 66.

death was too profound to be fully appreciated. Inherited teaching, it may be claimed, has less survival value than original creative discovery within a community.

(3) A stronger argument is the outright claim that it is in every way reasonable to suppose that Jesus Himself reflected upon the course and issues of His ministry, and, if so, must have made His interpretation the subject of teaching. This claim involves the perils of 'psychologizing', against which, in reaction to the work of the older liberals, we have frequently been warned. Danger, however, is not a sufficient deterrent in historical criticism, provided the investigator is alive to it. And it must be conceded that those who advance this claim have not a little to say for themselves. The oft-repeated argument, that the fate of the prophets, the death of John, and the presence of a bitter and growing opposition on the part of the Jewish hierarchy, prompted sombre reflections about the issues of the life and ministry of Jesus, has lost nothing of its force; and it is supported by His biting words, 'It cannot be that a prophet perish out of Jerusalem' (Luke 13:33). If He also foresaw the certainty of the destruction of Jerusalem (Mark 13:1f., Luke 13:34; 21:20–4)—a view for which a strong case can be made[1]—can He have gone to His tragic end without considering how it cohered with the order of God's providential purposes? Was Mark mistaken when he believed that Jesus was not overtaken by surprise? It will be said that this is subjective thinking; and certainly there is always a danger of reading one's own thoughts into any account of the career of Jesus. Again the danger is real, but those who accept the challenge are fortified by their refusal to believe that Gospel tradition was no more than a mass of isolated items and by their conviction that the primitive community contained ear- and eye-witnesses.

(4) The conservative view reaches its climax in the submission that no one was more likely than Jesus Himself to reinterpret the functions of 'the Son of Man' in terms of 'the Suffering Servant'. If this interpretation was that of a discerning individual, why should the insight not have been that of Jesus Himself? Can He have taken over the name 'Son of Man' without transforming its content in Daniel 7 and I Enoch?

[1] Cf. C. H. Dodd, *The Journal of Roman Studies*, xxxvi, 47–54.

This vulnerable line of thought can appeal to the allusive manner in which the language and ideas of Isaiah 53 are used in the Passion-sayings in contrast with Luke 22:37, which is by no means ruled out from consideration, and Matthew 8:17 and 12:18–21, which are editorial; and we are entitled to ask whether the conviction that 'the Son of Man must suffer' is not naturally expressed by Jesus Himself in the familiar language of Scripture.

Such are some of the arguments which require reconsideration in the light of the Servant Christology in the New Testament. It is perhaps too much to hope that anything like general agreement upon this question is probable in the foreseeable future, for the problem is nicely balanced and the Passion-sayings are a challenge to us as well as a puzzle. The purpose of this essay is to insist that the case for their genuineness must not go by default, and that all its aspects must be considered, especially that of the Servant Christology. For the student no task is so necessary in the study of the teaching of Jesus as that of setting conflicting arguments continually before the mind, in particular those with which he is inclined to disagree. Only so are settled convictions justifiable; for the one attitude which is fatal in facing problems is the closed mind which accepts the shibboleths of a passing day.

(*1955*)

V

The Alleged Neglect of M. Alfred Loisy

In a recent issue of the *Hibbert Journal*[1] Dr. Jacks has
instanced the neglect of British scholars to appreciate the
worth of M. Alfred Loisy as a New Testament critic. He thinks
that the work of the French school of critics, with M. Loisy
at its head, is little known in this country. The English or
American scholar is 'snowed under' by an avalanche of
German scholarship, and 'it is only here and there, among
critics who have allowed themselves a French holiday from
their German preoccupations, that the work of M. Loisy has
won any footing in this country.' Dr. Jacks thinks that we
cannot count on a perpetuity of this state of things. 'Loisy's
work is well known all over the continent of Europe, and it is
only a question of a few years before it becomes well known in
England and America.' Sooner or later the educated laity,
attracted by the charm and lucidity of Loisy's work, will
become acquainted with his conclusions, with especially
disastrous consequences for those who desire 'a creed in
harmony with modern thought.'

In certain respects Dr. Jacks is quite right about the alleged
neglect of M. Loisy. It is true that in most British 'surveys' of
the present state of New Testament criticism Loisy is 'left out
of the picture.' I believe he is right in saying that in *The Four
Gospels* Dr. Streeter does not refer to him, although on several
vital points Loisy's conclusions are in violent collision with
his own. He is certainly correct when he points out that, in
contrast with Harnack's works, Loisy's books (with one or
two minor exceptions) are left in the original. Now the really
pertinent matter is the meaning of this neglect, and here, I
think, issue must be joined with Dr. Jacks's diagnosis. It may
be that there are critics who have formed their estimate of

[1] Vol. xxiii., No. 4, pp. 577ff.

Loisy's worth on the basis of *L'Évangile et l'Église* and, in consequence, have neglected the commentaries written since his excommunication. If so, they have been caught napping. But on the whole the 'clerical scholars' of this country are not quite so ignorant of Loisy's work as Dr. Jacks imagines, and their failure to provide English translations is not 'due to an oversight'. I believe that the explanation lies latent in Dr. Jacks's estimate of M. Loisy: 'for there is no denying M. Loisy's significance as a critic of the New Testament.' So far as I know, few British New Testament scholars accept this rosy view.

I am well aware how hopelessly prejudiced such an opinion sounds. Loisy's conclusions are very radical, and to attempt to discredit his significance as a critic seems to be a particularly flagrant example of criticism conducted under the sound of 'church bells'. But one must not too readily submit to terrorism of this kind. I do not think that it is true that 'on the whole . . . Christian piety, in one or other of its many forms, remains in control of our critical investigations.' British New Testament scholars are not accustomed to reject conclusions merely because they do not like them. Their attitude to M. Loisy rests upon a reasoned estimate of the value of his work, and it is not necessary to be an expert to decide whether their estimate is just. In the present essay I propose to indicate some of the reasons which prevent most British critics from assigning to M. Loisy the significance which Dr. Jacks thinks he deserves.

I

In the article to which I have already referred Dr. Jacks has given an excellent summary of Loisy's position as regards the Acts of the Apostles. The attitude taken up towards the Third Gospel in Loisy's recent commentary *L'Évangile selon Luc* is much the same. The Gospel is held to be a composite work. It is a second century Christian expansion (A.D. 120–130) of a genuine writing of Luke, the companion of Paul, the latter having been written about A.D. 80 from materials supplied by Mark and the collection of Sayings of Jesus commonly known as 'Q'. The final redactor, whose aim throughout is apologetic, is identical with the writer to whom we owe the Acts in its present form.

The basis of this hypothesis is a definite attitude towards the Gospel writings. Loisy holds that no Gospel simply reflects the impression produced by the life and death of Jesus on those who were eyewitnesses.[1] The kind of tradition one naturally expects is lacking. What stands out most clearly is rather the poverty of the primitive recollections. The *légende* of Jesus is not a selection of historical reminiscences; it is a redaction of the Christological myth, elaborated on the basis of Old Testament texts, to meet the needs of faith in Jesus and to provide a defence of this faith against Jews.[2] Taking this view of the situation, Loisy finds it impossible to admit that Luke, the companion of Paul, can be the author of the two books to Theophilus in their entirety. He claims that the unity of the style does not preclude this view. The stylistic unity is the work of the redactor who has touched up and imitated Luke's style.

Is it possible, then, to recover the original work? Loisy's clue is the difference between that which the Prologues (Luke 1:1–4 and Acts 1:1–2) propose and what the two canonical works actually contain. In view of Luke 1:1–4, the 'first book to Theophilus' cannot have contained the Birth narratives nor again the narratives of the Resurrection at the end; the work probably ended with the words of the centurion at the death of Jesus. We cannot be certain that it contained the Preaching and Baptism of John nor the accounts of the Baptism and Temptation of Jesus. Probably the work began very much like Marcion's version: 'In the fifteenth year of the reign of Tiberius Cæsar Jesus went down to Capernaum . . .'. Luke 4:16–30 (the story of the Synagogue at Nazareth)

---

[1] 'Aucun évangile ne reflète simplement l'impression₎ produite par la vie et la mort du Christ sur ceux qui en ont été les témoins.' (*L'Évangile selon Luc*, p. 46.)

[2] 'En réalité, ce n'est pas d'une telle tradition qu'a vécu d'abord la foi, et l'extréme indigence des souvenirs primitifs est ce qui apparaît de plus clair: la légende de Jésus, dans son ensemble, n'est pas un choix de souvenirs historiques, c'est comme une réduction du mythe christologique élaboré sur les textes de l'Ancien Testament pour la satisfaction de la foi en Jésus et pour l'apologie de cette foi contre les Juifs; c'est l'expression même de cette foi dans une commémoration dramatique du Christ mourant et ressuscitant; et sous cette commémoration il n'est pas autrement facile de discerner ce qu'ont été, comme faits de l'histoire, la vie et la mort de Jésus . . .' (*op. cit*, pp. 45f.).

transposes and develops the story of Mark 6:1-6. It fore-shadows the rejection of the Jews and the open door to the Gentiles. In like manner the story of the Miraculous Draught of Fishes (Luke 5:1-11) delineates in symbolic form the rôle of Peter as the founder of the universal Church. Neither of these narratives can have belonged to Luke's first book, and this is true of the greater part of the matter which is peculiar to the canonical Gospel.

It must not be imagined, however, that the original book was a reliable historical work. Like its sources, Mark and 'Q', the 'first book to Theophilus' was *une légende sacrée*, in large measure the product and not the deposit of Apostolic traditions. The facts could not have been otherwise since the simple faith in Jesus was immediately transformed into faith in the Immortal Christ. Luke wrote with complete sincerity, but his 'accomplished facts' are acquisitions, the visions of the young faith in its crucified hero. This faith was unlatched (*déclenché*) by the personal action of Jesus, but the beginning has never been related apart from the faith it raised up.[1]

These far-reaching literary principles are announced—one cannot say that they are discussed—in a brief introductory section of nineteen pages 'La Composition du Troisieme Evangile', pp. 44-63). No attempt is made to discuss objections or the difficulties which arise if the hypothesis is valid. In the remainder of the present essay I propose to examine some of these difficulties and then to consider broader criticisms in relation to M. Loisy as a commentator.

II

(1) The first obvious point of criticism is the lack of any kind of external evidence pointing to Loisy's proposed reconstruction of the Gospel. How is it that early Christian tradition knows nothing of this recasting of Luke's original work half a century after its composition? It is past belief that so extensive an editorial process can have left no ripple. One need not demand a discussion of the question by Irenæus or Eusebius, but it is incredible that in early citations of the Gospel all

---

[1] 'L'action personnelle de Jésus a déclenché la foi; mais ce commencement n'a jamais été raconté indépendament de la foi qu'il avait suscitée' (*op. cit.*, p. 55).

signs of the double edition should be lacking. Was not this the line followed by Blass? It would be entirely futile to urge as an explanation the satisfaction which the canonical expansion would yield to contemporary needs. No one with a reputation to lose would suggest the deliberate suppression of Luke's earlier work. Textual evidence pointing to the extensive redactional process could not have been suppressed.

(2) In the second place objection must be taken to M. Loisy's treatment of the stylistic problem. He cleverly explains the unity of the style by ascribing this to the final redactor, but does he not overreach himself in this contention? Seams, sutures, peculiarities of construction and vocabulary are common features in cases where editorial elaboration is to be suspected. These are found in the canonical ending of Mark (16:9–20), in the Fourth Gospel, the Apocalypse and in Romans. Why should it be otherwise in Luke? How is it that Loisy's redactor is so successful? Granted, for argument's sake, that the style of the whole is his, why are there no lurking traces of the style of his predecessor? Loisy is in no doubt about the extensive additions of his redactor and without hesitation can lay his finger upon them. Ought not these large redactorial passages to possess some linguistic individuality of style which might serve as a kind of criterion? Would it not be reasonable to look out for cases where the editorial conscience slept and for others where the original material proved intractable? We do not require M. Loisy, or anyone else, to prove his case by a linguistic argument, but we do seriously ask if his avoidance of the issue is not gratuitous.

It is true that in his introduction Loisy has a section on the literary form of the Gospel, but in it he nowhere comes to grips with the difficulties mentioned above. The alleged rhythmical style is a matter which affects his translation of the Gospel, not his treatment of its literary construction. The nearest approach to the latter is the suggestion that the secondary Semitisms are those of a man who knew no Hebrew, although Luke, if he was a physician of Antioch, must have known at least Aramaic.[1] But Loisy does not tie himself down

[1] 'Force est de constater que ses nombreux hébraïsmes sont d'un homme qui ne savait pas l'hébreu, mais cultivait la version des Septante, quoique Luc, s'il a été médecin à Antioche, ait dû savoir au moins l'araméen' (*op. cit.*, p. 63).

to the opinion that the style is that of a physician. On the contrary, he observes that the vocabulary of the Acts (27) is more that of a sailor than that of a disciple of Hippocrates.

(3) Turning to the redactional hypothesis, we may notice several points in which its employment is open to criticism.

Loisy does not spare his redactor. His story of the Visit to the Temple is said to be *une médiocre fiction* (p. 131), while his additions to the story of the Centurion's Servant are 'child's play' (enfantillages), difficult to credit to Luke (p. 216). The healings recorded when the messengers of John came to Jesus (Luke 7:21) are *pure fiction* (p. 223), while the reference to the soldiers who addressed the Baptist is dismissed by the remark that 'our redactor has a certain weakness (*faible*) for soldiers' (p. 138). These are fair examples of M. Loisy in the rôle of a commentator, and reveal his estimate of the mentality of his redactor. All the more remarkable is it to find that this same person is capable of insinuating into his fictions the most delicate of editorial subtleties. In the account of the Miraculous Draught, for example, 'Jesus in the boat, teaching Galileans, represents the preaching of the Gospel to the Jews,' while the order given to Simon to advance into the open sea, and the abundant catch which follows, 'represent the preaching to the Gentiles' (p. 175). The story of the Widow's Son, at Nain, prefigures the salvation of Israel, just as the account of the Centurion's Servant prefigures the salvation of Gentiles (p. 220). A particularly illuminating example of the redactor's editorial dexterity is to be found in the Visit of Jesus to the Village of Martha and Mary. The unsophisticated reader is impressed with the natural charm of this story and its claim to be regarded as a genuine recollection of the ministry of Jesus. But in Loisy's hands the two sisters are meant by the redactor to be the representatives of the two sections of the primitive Church, the Judæo-Christian and the Hellenistic-Christian parties. Even the parable of the Good Samaritan does not escape. Here the redactor has expanded a Jewish story in order to show the superiority of the true Christian over the proud Jew in the fulfilment of the Law. Is not all this criticism run to seed?

Postponing this conclusion, one may notice the opportunities the redactor has missed and the features he has left untouched.

How is it that so virile a portraiture of Jesus still lingers in this
second century compilation? Why is omniscience never
predicated of the Lukan Jesus? Why does He offer unavailing
prayer (22:32), and long for what is impossible on earth
(22:15)? Why does He so rarely quote the Old Testament
in relation to Himself, never using anything like the Matthæan
formula: 'that it might be fulfilled which was spoken by the
prophet'? Surely the redactor has sometimes nodded! What
a chance he missed in his elaboration of the story of the
Woman in the City (7:36–50)! The woman is forgiven because
of her faith—so far he works according to plan. But why did
he not relate her faith to the personality of Jesus? Why, indeed,
in the Third Gospel is no one ever saved because he believes
in Jesus? Salvation comes to Zacchæus; but for some unknown
reason the redactor's allegorical preoccupations have not led
him to ascribe to the publican any confession of Jesus as Lord.
The more one thinks about Loisy's hypothetical redactor the
more wraith-like he becomes; he has left undone the things
he ought to have done and there is no health in him.

But our present difficulties are not ended. Neither Loisy
nor anyone else can make the Lukan Christology less primitive
than it is; and yet we are to set this down to the account of a
writer in the third decade of the second century! According
to Loisy the redactor has read the Fourth Gospel, yet he has
left us a Christology which substantially is not more than
'pre-Pauline Gentile Christianity.'[1] The Sonship of Christ, for
example, is scarcely more than moral and volitional. Nowhere,
not even in 22:29 and 34:49, is a metaphysical Sonship
predicated to Him. The Lukan Christology is naturally
explained if it belongs to the third quarter of the first century;
in the second century it is an anachronism.

It will be seen from the foregoing that Loisy's theory is
anything but self-consistent. It is also open to the charge of
redundancy. No more than the canonical Luke is the 'first
book to Theophilus,' according to Loisy, a historical work.
Like the redactor's compilation it also is *une légende du culte,
en grande partie produit et non souvenir de la tradition apostolique
invoquée par l'auteur du prologue* (p. 55). What then, we may ask,
becomes of the principle by which the two editions are

[1] Cf. Streeter, *The Four Gospels*, p. 556.

distinguished? Has not Loisy accepted as a partition-clue the very characteristics which he finds in the original work of Luke?

(4) It remains for us, finally, to consider the critical principle itself. Is it a just view of the Third Gospel to treat it as the creation of the Christian Faith,[1] and in no sense a historical work?

It seems to me that whatever plausibility this opinion has springs from the truth which it exploits. It is undeniable that the Gospels reflect the times in which they were written. No serious New Testament critic doubts this. Even critics with 'clerical affiliations' find illustrations of later preoccupations in the Matthæan story of the Watch at the Tomb, the corporeal traits in the Resurrection narratives, the Birth Stories, and perhaps the Nature Miracles, although on some of these points many of them prefer to keep an open mind. But because one finds the reaction of the Christian Faith upon the contents of the Gospels, is it necessary to suppose that they have lost all contact with the original facts and are no more than the creations of Christological fancy? Stripped of all fine phrases, it is to this pass that Loisy has reduced Renan's 'most beautiful book in the world'. On this view the yawning gulf between the Synoptics and the Fourth Gospel becomes an enigma. Less mystical than the Fourth Evangelist, as the latter is conceived by liberal critics, Loisy's redactor has succeeded in investing his fictions with the verisimilitude of history!

It is more than doubtful if we can give a credible background to the hypothetical redactor. One of his main purposes is by the aid of his creations to teach the universality of the message of salvation—the open door to Gentiles as well as Jews. In A.D. 120–130 such a redactor is a sub-apostolic Rip Van Winkle. Had not the battle long been won by Paul? So conclusive, indeed, was the victory, that in the second century Paul stands in the background, eclipsed by the brilliance of his great achievements. How can we with any conviction presuppose a second century redactor, concerned to rehabilitate

---

[1] 'Nulle part cette vie n'est celle de la simple doctrine perçue par un auditeur attentif, du simple fait regardé par un spectateur curieux; c'est celle d'une foi qui s'affirme et qui se defend, qui se définit et se figure liturgiquement, qui se réalise elle-même dans les créations qu'elle anime de son esprit' (*op. cit.*, p. 62).

Luke's original Gospel in order to teach the elementary applications of Paulinism? It may justly be suspected that it is not so much the historical character of the Gospel which is in doubt as that of the redactor himself. Certainly it requires a greater faith to accept him as a creature of flesh and blood than it does to treat Martha and Mary, Zacchæus and the Penitent Thief as historical personages.

III

In the light of what has already been said the attitude of most British scholars to M. Loisy as a critic of the New Testament will be more readily understood. But in addition to the special points which may be urged against his hypothesis in *L'Evangile selon Luc*, there are several matters of a broader kind which need to be taken into account. These also may explain why in various 'surveys' of 'the present state of New Testament criticism' M. Loisy is, in the words of Dr. Jacks, 'left out of the picture'.

In this connexion Loisy's literary output during the last six years is worthy of notice. Since 1920, apart from articles, he has published six or seven considerable volumes, embracing at least 4,500 pages, and treating in detail the Acts, the Third and the Fourth Gospels, the Apocalypse, and a translation and general introduction to the New Testament. In England we can show nothing to equal this industry, and I doubt if Germany can. Even the work of R. H. Charles seems leisurely when compared with Loisy's, for the composition of Charles's commentary on the Apocalypse covered over twenty-five years, though it was preceded by a series of works on allied subjects. Compared with Loisy, Canon Streeter is a tortoise, while the late Dr. V. H. Stanton moved with the pace of a snail. You can carry Sir John Hawkins's works in one hand; to move Loisy's books you must summon a porter. Now it may seriously be doubted if scientific works can be reproduced like Waverley Novels. Commentaries, if they are to be of any worth, demand hours of research and close acquaintance with the writings of other critics. Many questions must be weighed again and again, and sometimes when all has been done they must be left open. Now on all these points, except the first, M. Loisy is exposed to criticism. There can be no doubt at all that he has a close and first-hand knowledge of the minutiæ of New Testament problems. He has carefully weighed the agreements and the differences between the synoptic writers and the significance of the textual variants. As regards the detailed history of critical opinion, one must speak with less confidence. In *L'Évangile selon Luc*, for example, this topic is confined to twelve pages, which contain no more than can be found in any modest manual of New Testament Introduction. Ramsay and Moffatt are not mentioned and there are only passing references to Hawkins and Streeter. What is more vital is the manner in which the work of exposition is conducted. A comparison with R. H. Charles will show what I have in mind. In the commentary on the Apocalypse you can see not only what Charles himself thinks, but what Wellhausen, Spitta, Erbes, Bousset, Loisy and others have taught. You can see what Charles has accepted from these writers, what he rejects, and why. One has a right to expect this, but in Loisy's volumes you find little or nothing of the kind. Loisy crowds his own stage; in the body of his works you hear few opinions except his own. He rarely hesitates and little is obscure to him. No doubt this adds something to the charm of his work, but in the eyes of British scholars it does not enhance 'his significance as a critic of the New Testament'. A critic who never loses the scent is not really following it.

The strongest point in the indictment is Loisy's failure to discuss his own critical principles. He announces these again and again, as the quotations in the present essay will show. He makes it perfectly clear what his redactional hypothesis looks like when it is erected, but you never see the foundations or the subsoil. In a word, you do not get a detailed discussion of the opinion that the Third Gospel is a book of the Christian cult. For the detailed treatment of this foundation principle fifty pages would not have been too many in a commentary consisting of six hundred pages. But Loisy does not supply this; he prefers the method of emphatic reiteration, in which he is a past master. To say, then, that his work lacks objective basis is no more than simple truth. Loisy is not the first critic to suggest a double edition of the Third Gospel. In this matter he has been preceded by Blass and by Streeter, though in the case of these scholars the two versions are thought to be the work of Luke himself. In contrast with Loisy, each of these scholars bases his hypothesis upon objective facts: Blass upon textual phenomena; Streeter mainly upon the disposition of Markan and non-Markan matter within the Gospel. Loisy's critical methods are entirely different. His hypothesis does not rest upon a series of facts found within the Gospel. The Gospel is read in the light of a theory of Gospel Origins antecedently held, persistently announced, and never fully discussed. The result is that his commentary is not so much a discussion of the Gospel according to Luke as of Luke according to Loisy.

When we get down to the bottom, it is a feeling of this kind, more or less conscious, which accounts for the neglect of Loisy in this country; it is not a matter of prejudice, or fear, or ignorance, but a fundamental distrust of his critical methods. In England Loisy's commentaries are read with the greatest interest—but in order to see what he says about the Gospels, not to understand them. For this reason those scholars who are anxious to find a creed in harmony with modern thought do not discover in M. Loisy the difficulty which Dr. Jacks supposes. Why should they consider too seriously a scholar whose main claim for consideration is a felicitous style and an ability to tell us what he thinks?

(1926)

VI

Does the New Testament call Jesus 'God'?

THIS IS A QUESTION of considerable importance since it not only concerns the interpretation of a number of New Testament passages, but also bears on the modern problems of Christology. It should be recognized at the outset that the question is not whether Jesus is divine, but whether He is actually described as Θεός, and whether we of today are justified in speaking of Him as 'God'. Some scholars do speak of Him in this way, while others who hold the highest estimate of His Person hesitate to use this name and feel a sense of uneasiness when they hear it applied to Him. By way of example we may compare the way in which Professor Leonard Hodgson speaks of Jesus in his Gifford Lectures, *For Faith and Freedom*, and the usage of Professor James Denney discussed in his correspondence with Sir W. Robertson Nicoll as revealed in the *Letters of Principal James Denney to W. Robertson Nicoll* [1883–1917], 120–126.

Professor Hodgson says that the life of Christ was the life of One for whom we can find no place in our thought 'short of acknowledging Him as God', and again that we cannot account for what He was and did by thinking of Him 'as anything less than God' (pp. 83–86). In a letter to Principal Denney, Robertson Nicoll said that, for all his apparent orthodoxy, there was a singular vein of scepticism in Denney, and Denney admitted that the aversion he had to such expressions as 'Jesus is God' was linguistic as much as theological. 'Jesus', he wrote, 'is man as well as God, in some way therefore both less and more than God; and consequently a form of proposition which in our idiom suggests inevitably the precise equivalence of Jesus and God does some kind of injustice to the "truth" ' (p. 57).

The contrast between these two points of view is very marked, and it must be considered which of them commands the greater support on exegetical and theological grounds.

I

The relevant New Testament passages are comparatively few. Bultmann observes that in describing Christ as "God" the New Testament still exercises great restraint. 'Except for John 1:1', Bultmann observes, 'where the pre-existent Logos is called God, and John 20:28, where Thomas reverences the risen Christ with the exclamation, "My Lord and my God" this assertion is made—at least by any probable exegesis—only in 2 Thessalonians 1:12, Titus 2:13, and 2 Peter 1:1'. To these he adds in a footnote, 'The doxology in Romans 9:5 is scarcely to be referred to Christ; in John 1:18 and 1 Timothy 3:16 "God" is a secondary variant.' These last named passages cannot be dismissed so easily. All these passages must be examined. Meantime we may note that he says that Ignatius, on the contrary, speaks of Christ as God as if it were a thing to be taken for granted, in such phrases as 'God manifested himself as man' (Ephesians 19:3), 'God's blood' (Ephesians 1:1), 'the bread of God, that is, the flesh of Jesus Christ' (Romans 7:3). As early, then, as the first decade of the second century this custom of speaking of Christ as 'God' was beginning to spread.

In examining the New Testament passages we may with advantage begin with the earliest, Romans 9:5. It stands as the climax of a list of privileges possessed by the Jews, and in the Revised Version reads as follows: 'And of whom is Christ as concerning the flesh, who is over all, God blessed for ever. Amen.' In this Version Christ is described as God, but in the margin two alternative renderings are given in which the closing words read, 'He who is God over all be (is) blessed for ever', or after the word 'flesh', and so with reference to Christ, 'who is over all. God be (is) blessed for ever'. The American Revised Standard Version reverses the arrangement and has the doxology to God in the text. Moffatt does the same.

It is well known that the greatest of the commentators range themselves on each side, Sanday and Headlam, G. G. Findlay, P. C. Boylan, and many others in relating the doxology to Christ, but others, including H. A. W. Meyer, J. Denney, C. A. Anderson Scott, C. H. Dodd, and other commentators in maintaining that it is addressed to God. The dispute continues. Among more recent commentators Anders Nygren defends the rendering of the Revised Version, but Bultmann, J. Knox, and C. K. Barrett refer the doxology to God. For my own part I think the balance of opinion falls on this side, and that Christ is not addressed as God. As so many have observed, Barrett contends that nowhere else does Paul call Christ God. 'Philippians 2:6', he says, 'is not a real parallel.' 'Is it likely', he asks, 'that he would here run counter to his general practice?', although he admits that it is not impossible. The New English Bible reads, 'May God, supreme above all, be blessed for ever! Amen.'

The only other Pauline passage which has been claimed as a reference to Christ as God is 2 Thessalonians 1:12, 'according to the grace of our God and the Lord Jesus Christ', but this interpretation is so dubious that some commentators do not even mention it. It is manifest that Paul is speaking first of God and secondly of Christ.[1]

A single passage in the Epistle to the Hebrews may be mentioned, but it supplies no ground at all for the supposition that the author thought and spoke of Christ as God. The passage is a quotation from Psalm 45:7–8 in Hebrews 1:8–9 which is applied to Christ, to show His superiority to the angels.

But of the Son he saith,
Thy throne, O God, is for ever and ever;
And the sceptre of uprightness is the sceptre of thy kingdom.
Thou hast loved righteousness, and hated iniquity;
Therefore God, thy God, hath anointed thee
With the oil of gladness above thy fellows.

The Psalm is Messianic and the divine name is carried over with the rest of the quotation. Like Paul and John the writer frequently uses the name 'the Son', and he does so in introducing this very quotation. He has no intention of suggesting that Jesus is God.

We reach a more difficult issue in the Gospel of John. Here, in the Prologue, the Word is said to be God, but, as often observed, in contrast with the clause, 'the Word was with God', the definite article is not used (in the final clause). For this reason it is generally translated 'and the Word was divine' (Moffatt) or is not regarded as God in the absolute sense of

[1] Cf. Dr. Leon Morris, *The Epistles of Paul to the Thessalonians*, 123.

the name. The New English Bible neatly paraphrases the phrase in the words 'and what God was, the Word was.' In a second passage in the Prologue (1:18) the textual evidence attests 'only-begotten God' more strongly than 'only-begotten Son', but the latter is preferred by many commentators as being more in harmony with Johannine usage and with the succeeding clause, 'who is in the bosom of the Father'. In neither passage is Jesus unequivocally called God, while again and again in the Gospel He is named 'the Son' or 'the Son of God'. In a third passage, however, there is no doubt that the name 'God' is assigned to Him. When Thomas is bidden to see the hands and side of Jesus, he cries in adoring love, 'My Lord and my God'. This cry is spontaneous and devotional and illustrates an aspect, and not the whole, of the Evangelist's Christology. Like the author of Hebrews he thinks and speaks of Christ in the category of Sonship.

In the Fourth Gospel we approach nearest to the use of Θεός as a Christological title. Two late passages, however, must be mentioned in which the application of the name is dubious. The first is Titus 2:13, 'looking for the blessed hope and appearing of the glory of our great God and Saviour Jesus Christ'. Much discussion has centred upon this passage. The point at issue is whether the Greek should be rendered 'the glory of our great God-and-Saviour, Jesus Christ', or '. . . of the great God, and of our Saviour Jesus Christ.' The grammarians range themselves on both sides, for in *koiné* Greek the rendering of the article with 'Saviour' is possible even when it is not actually repeated. The theologians are also divided. The New English Bible has 'the splendour of our great God and Saviour Christ Jesus'. In a non-Pauline writing of late date this translation is quite possible, but it is not certain. A similar situation is present in the second passage, 2 Peter 1:1, in the phrase 'the righteousness of our God and Saviour Jesus Christ' (NEB, 'the justice of our God and Saviour Jesus Christ'), but here again alternatives which distinguish two Persons are possible. The issue is even less important in view of the fact that 2 Peter is a pseudonymous writing later in date than the time of Ignatius.

All the relevant passages have been mentioned and we may accept Bultmann's words as an understatement, 'In describing

Christ as "God" the New Testament still exercises great restraint.'

The reasons for this restraint are not far to seek. It is due in large measure to the profound effect of the monotheism of the Old Testament upon the New Testament writers. I have said elsewhere of Paul's Christology, 'He will not compromise his belief that God is One God, not even for Christ's sake',[1] and this is true also of the author of Hebrews and John. It is also due to the fact that in the New Testament period the time has not yet come to define the relationships which exist between the Father and the Son. If they are not defined, neither are they obscured. 'Only-begotten' is as far as John is prepared to go.

II

The question may be asked. What is the value of the inquiry we are making? Are the names we assign to Jesus Christ of practical importance, or is their interest merely academic? I have no doubt that their importance is very great indeed. First, the habit of calling Jesus God tends to restrict unduly our understanding of the riches of the Divine Being. We stand on a slippery slope which may easily lead to a Sabellian interpretation of the Person of Christ. I do not mean that all who speak of Christ in this way are Sabellianist in theology, but that this is the tendency of their Christology. The widespread, but probably doubtful, rendering of 2 Corinthians 5:19, 'God was in Christ, reconciling the world unto himself', is perhaps a sign of this tendency. The margin of the New English Bible translates the passage much better, 'God was reconciling the world to. himself by Christ.' Doubtless each Person of the Trinity is interpermeated by the other Persons, so that it can be said with Paul, 'For it is in Christ that the complete being of the Godhead dwells' (Colossians 2:9 [NEB]), but nowhere else does the Apostle speak of the divine indwelling in Him. He appears to avoid the language of immanence when speaking of Christ. And rightly, for to describe Christ as God is to neglect the sense in which He is both less and more, man as well as God within the glory and limitations of His Incarnation.

[1] Cf. V. Taylor, *The Person of Christ in New Testament Teaching*, 60.

Secondly, then, the wonder of the Incarnation is compromised. It is well known that the New Testament does not hesitate to describe Jesus as a man. Paul does this in Romans 5:15 and Philippians 2:8, and the author of the Pastoral Epistles in 1 Timothy 2:5. Now if we call Jesus God, we may find it difficult to refer to Him as a man, that is, if by this term we mean a separate individual. We may prefer to think and speak of Him as Man. In a well-known passage in *Atonement and Personality* R. C. Moberly wrote, 'If He might have been, yet He certainly was not, a man only, amongst men. His relation to the human race is not that He was another specimen, differing, by being another, from everyone except Himself. His relation to the race was not a differentiating but a consummating relation. He was not generically, but inclusively, man' (p. 86). *Atonement and Personality* is a great theological classic, but this particular argument is an example of losing the substance when grasping at the shadow. 'Man', in the sense in which Moberly uses the term, is a meaningless abstraction. It is part of the price we have to pay when speaking of Christ as 'God'.

And this is not all. The Gospels clearly show that the knowledge of Jesus was limited, that He asked questions for the sake of information, that His understanding of Nature and the world was that of His day, that He challenged the rich ruler who addressed Him as 'Good Master' with the question, 'Why do you call me good? No one is good except God alone.' These issues have constantly caused embarrassment[1] and must continue to do so if without qualification Jesus is described as God. Honest historical criticism becomes very difficult on this basis, and what is even more important, no fitting grasp of the reality and depth of the self-emptying of Jesus is possible. It might be thought that, in using restraint in speaking of the Deity of Christ, we are robbing Him of His true dignity, but so far from doing this, we are *enhancing* it, since it is of the nature of Deity that it can stoop to the depth of man's need in a sacrifice to which there is no parallel. The one clear ascription of Deity to Christ, 'My Lord and my God', in the New Testament is addressed to Him in His Risen and Exalted life,

---

[1] I have discussed the most important alternative views in my commentary on Mark, *The Gospel according to St. Mark*, 426f.

and breathes the atmosphere of worship. This is the sphere to which it belongs, but we are most likely to kneel in adoration if we have first entered into the truth of the words, 'For the divine nature was his from the first; yet he did not think to snatch at equality with God, but made himself nothing, assuming the nature of a slave. Bearing the human likeness, revealed in human shape, he humbled himself, and in obedience accepted even death—death on a cross' (Philippians 2:6–9 [NEB]).

(1962)

VII

The Order of Q

IN VIEW of current strictures[1] upon the Q hypothesis it may
be of advantage to reconsider one of the arguments by which
hitherto it has been supported. This study does not pretend
to examine the case for the hypothesis as a whole, but only
the question of order in the parallel passages in Matthew and
Luke.

The argument from order is often supported by printing
passages in two columns, with the Lukan parallels on the left
and the Matthaean parallels on the right, as may be seen in
any good textbook. These lists are certainly not unimpressive.
One can see at a glance sequences which point to a common
order derived from the hypothetical source. Unfortunately,
however, marked variations of order are also visible, and,
accordingly, the argument is to this extent at a discount. I
propose to show that the common order is much more impressive that it appears to be, and is, in fact, a very strong argument
indeed.

There are several reasons why the lists, as usually presented,
conceal the signs of a common order. First, the lists often
include a number of passages in which the linguistic agreement
between Matthew and Luke is relatively small, especially in
parabolic material, and in which by wide consent Matthew,
while possibly using Q, is dependent on a second source other
than Q. These passages (Group A) include the following:

The saying on the Great Commandment,
   Luke 10:25–28 (Matthew 22:34–39).

[1] Cf. B. C. Butler, *The Originality of Matthew, passim*, who claims that Q is 'an
unnecessary and vicious hypothesis' (p. 170); A. M. Farrer, *Journal of Theological
Studies*, N.S., iii. 102–6, who twice observes that Abbot Butler 'demolishes the Q
hypothesis' (pp. 102, 106).

The saying on the Signs of the Times,
  Luke 12:54–56 (Matthew 16:2f.).
The saying on the Narrow Gate,
  Luke 13:23f. (Matthew 7:13f.).
The saying on the Shut Door,
  Luke 13:25–27 (Matthew 7:22f.; 25:10–12)
The parable of the Great Supper,
  Luke 14:15–24 (Matthew 22:1–10).
The parable of the Lost Sheep,
  Luke 15:4–7, 10 (Matthew 18:12–14).
The parable of the Pounds,
  Luke 19:12–27 (Matthew 25:14–30).

If, in these passages, Q and another source overlapped, it is reasonable to expect that the order of Q, as reflected in Matthew and Luke, may be obscured.

Secondly, the usual lists include short isolated sayings which, for editorial reasons, either Evangelist, but presumably Matthew, might be disposed to insert in another context. These passages (Group B) include:

Luke 6:31 (Matthew 7:12); Luke 6:39 (Matthew 15:14); Luke 6:40 (Matthew 10:24f.); Luke 10:16 (Matthew 10:40); Luke 11:33 (Matthew 5:15); Luke 12:10 (Matthew 12:32); Luke 12:11f. (Matthew 10:19f.); Luke 12:33f. (Matthew 6:20f.); Luke 14:11 and the doublet in 18:14b (Matthew 23:12 and the doublet in 18:4); Luke 16:13 (Matthew 6:24); Luke 16:16 (Matthew 11:12f.); Luke 16:17 (Matthew 5:18); Luke 16:18 (Matthew 5:32); Luke 22:30b (Matthew 19:28b).

Here again in some cases the use by Matthew of another source than Q (in whole or in part) may also be a disturbing factor.

Thirdly, the impressiveness of the lists suffers because Matthew has arranged the sayings and parables in five groups, 5–7, 10, 13, 18, 23–25. This editorial purpose is bound to have its effect in lists of parallel passages in Matthew and Luke. Indeed, in the light of it, it is remarkable that the lists display as much similarity in respect of order as actually appears.

The explanation of the diversities of order suggested above is reasonable. It must, however, be allowed that, as hitherto presented, it has the appearance of an apology; it looks like an attempt to make the best of a not very convincing case. In these circumstances it is desirable to attempt a new arrangement of the parallel passages, which will take into account the considerations mentioned above and, particularly, Matthew's editorial methods. Such a list is presented below. As will be seen, it includes seven columns instead of two. The Lukan passages are printed on the left and the Matthaean passages on the right, but in six columns: (1) those in Matthew 5–7; (2) those in Matthew 10; (3) in Matthew 13; (4) in Matthew 18; (5) in Matthew 23–25, and (6) in the rest of Matthew. I have omitted all the passages in Group A for reasons already given. I do not deny that most of these passages stood in Q, probably in their Lukan form, and that in them Matthew also has used Q, although to a very limited degree. In these passages, however, Matthew's main debt was to sources other than Q. For similar reasons Group B might have been omitted, but in these passages source criticism is more speculative, and it has seemed better to include all of them in the lists and to discuss separately those among them which visibly disturb sequences. These passages are enclosed in brackets and an asterisk is added in cases where conflation is possible and even probable. The vertical lines indicate sequences, that is, groups of passages, which stand in the same order in Matthew and in Luke. Presented in this way the table of parallel passages is as follows:

Parallel passages in Matthew and Luke suggestive of the use of the document Q

Luke	Matthew 5–7	Matthew 10	Matthew 13	Matthew 18	Matthew 23–25	Rest of Matthew
3:7–9, 16f.						3:7–12
3:21f.						3:16f.
4:1–13						4:1–11
6:20–23	5:3–6, 11f.					
6:27–30	5:39–44					
6:31	(7:12)					
6:32–36	5:45–48					
6:37f.	7:1f.					
6:39						(15:14)*
6:40		(10:24f)*				
6:41f.	7:3–5					
6:43–45	7:16–20					12:33–35
6:46	7:21					
6:47–49	7:24–27					

Luke	Matthew 5–7	Matthew 10	Matthew 13	Matthew 18	Matthew 23–25	Rest of Matthew
7:1–10						8:5–10, 13
7:18–23						11:2–6
7:24–28						11:7–11
7:31–35						11:16–19
9:57–60						8:19–22
10:2						9:37f.
10:3–12		10:9–16*				
10:13–15						11:21–23
10:16		(10:40)*				
10:21f.						11:25–27
10:23f.			13:16f.			
11:2–4	6:9–13					
11:9–13	7:7–11					
11:14–23						12:22–30
11:24–26						12:43–45
11:29–32						12:38–42
11:33	(5:15)*					
11:34f.	6:22f.					
11:49–51					23:34–36	
12:2f.		10:26f.				
12:4–7		10:28–31				
12:8f.		10:32f.				
12:10						(12:32)*
12:11f.		(10:19f.)*				
12:22–31	6:25–33					
12:33b, 34	(6:20f.)*					
12:39–46					24:43–51	
12:51–53		10:34–36				
12:57–59	5:25f.					
13:18–21			13:31–33			
13:28f.						8:11f.
13:34f.					23:37–39	
14:11				(18:4)*		
14:26f.		10:37f.				
16:13	(6:24)					
16:16						(11:12f.)
16:17	(5:18)					
16:18	(5:32)					
17:1f.				18:6f.		
17:3f.				18:15, 21f.		
17:5f.						17:20
17:23f.					24:26f.	
17:26f.					24:37–39	
17:33f.		10:39				
17:34f.					24:40	
17:37					(24:28)	19:28b
22:30b						

Notes:

1. It is not suggested that the above table is the whole of Q. It lacks the passages in Group A, which in their Lukan form are commonly assigned to Q, amounting to 43 verses. In all, the table includes about 194 verses.

Conclusions

The table strongly suggests that either (*a*) one Evangelist used the Gospel of the other, or (*b*) both Evangelists used a common documentary source. The long-abandoned hypothesis that Luke is dependent upon Matthew is sometimes tentatively suggested by modern scholars, but no one ventures to state a case which meets obvious objections.[1] Coupled with the other arguments[2] in favour of Q, the manifest signs of a common order in Matthew and Luke raise the hypothesis to a remarkable degree of cogency, short only of demonstration.[3] Of current suggestions regarding the demise of the Q hypothesis we may say, as Mark Twain said of premature announcements of his death, that they have been greatly exaggerated.

Notes (continued):

2. It lacks passages in Luke which have no parallel in Matthew but may none the less have been taken from Q, namely, Luke 6:24–26; 9:61f.; 12:35–38, 47f.

3. If desired, the parallels may be described as 'Q', that is, a list of passages common to Matthew and Luke.

4. Q may itself be compilation, but this is a possibility to be considered apart from the significance of 'Q'.

5. The parallels to Luke 14:11 (Luke 18:14b) and Matthew 18:4 (Matthew 23:12) are not included in the table.

6. It is to be observed that in Matthew 13 and 18 the sequences run throughout, whereas in the remaining columns of Matthew it is a question of group-sequences which often begin with the same chapters (5, 8, 23).

---

[1] Including the 122 translation-variants which Bussmann has noted in his source R. Cf. *Synoptische Studien*, ii. 151–5.

[2] The high percentage of agreement in very many of the parallel passages, the significance of doublets, and the presence of translation-variants.

[3] Of the ten Matthaean passages in the table which do not belong to a group-sequence, 12:38–42 is only an apparent exception, being a case of simple inversion for editorial reasons. Matthew 12:33–35 is a doublet of 7:16–20. The remaining eight passages are included in Class B mentioned above (Lukan parallels: 6:31, 39, 40; 11:33; 12:10, 11f.; 22:30b). In all these cases, except the first, there is reason to think that Matthew is not solely dependent on Q.

(1953)

VIII

The Original Order of Q*

IN VIEW OF the great contribution which Professor T. W. Manson has made to the study of Q, a contribution for which all students of Gospel origins are deeply grateful, it seems not inappropriate to offer in this essay a few comments on the order of this source. There are several reasons why such an investigation is desirable. First, it will be agreed that, while many important contributions have been made to this question, the results cannot be regarded as completely satisfactory. Again, and not unconnected with this situation, there has been a shift of interest which has caused a temporary halt to these discussions. For something like a generation the earlier interest in literary criticism, so virile during the latter part of the nineteenth century and the opening decades of the twentieth, has abated owing to the competing claims of Form Criticism, New Testament Theology, Typology, and existentialist assessments of the Gospel tradition. These newer and fruitful interests are not to be regretted and it was perhaps necessary that the well-tilled fields of literary criticism should lie fallow for a time. Nevertheless, it seems necessary, without neglecting the later disciplines, to return to the study of the older problems and to consider how far they are capable of a solution. Further, in the interval, the existence of Q has been vigorously assailed, notably by such scholars as E. Lummis,[1] H. G. Jameson,[2] B. C. Butler,[3] and A. Farrer.[4] These scholars have revived the hypothesis that Luke used the Gospel of Matthew as a source, and Abbot Butler has gone so far as to describe Q as 'an

---

*First published in A. J. B. Higgins ed. *New Testament Essays: Studies in Memory of T. W. Manson, 1893–1958*, Manchester University Press, and reprinted here by permission of the publishers.

[1] *How Luke was Written* (1915).
[2] *The Origin of the Synoptic Gospels* (1922).
[3] *The Originality of St. Matthew* (1951).
[4] *A Study in St. Mark* (1951).

unnecessary and vicious hypothesis'.[1] The Two Document
Hypothesis has been strongly attacked. These attacks have not
changed the views of its advocates, but in some quarters a
certain uneasiness is manifest. There is a tendency to speak of
Q as 'a hypothetical document' and its alleged unity has been
questioned.[2] On the other hand, there has been what must be
described as a closer approach to the Q Hypothesis on the part
of some Roman Catholic scholars. In the new *Catholic Commentary on Holy Scripture* (1953) Père Benoit has maintained
that an original Aramaic Gospel of Matthew was used as a
source by the three Synoptists. Similarly Dr. Alfred Wiken-
hauser,[3] who maintains that the Greek Matthew and Luke are
both dependent on Mark, suggests that Matthew composed the
logia in Aramaic, the Greek translation being the common
source used in the Greek Matthew and Luke.

In these circumstances it may be timely to re-examine the
order of Q in its bearings on the Q Hypothesis. At any rate
this is the theme of the present essay.

I

In this inquiry I shall use the symbol Q to represent those
sayings and parables in Matthew and Luke which are commonly
assigned to this source, accepting the view that Q was a
document as 'a working hypothesis'. I shall leave aside the
possibility that Q was preceded by earlier groups of sayings
and examine the common source which, by hypothesis, lay
before them as a unity. Several arguments have been held to
support this hypothesis—the linguistic agreements between
Matthew and Luke, the order reflected by the sayings, and the
presence of doublets in the two Gospels which point to the use
of Mark and at least one other source. I do not propose to
discuss all these arguments, but only the question of order,
which in many respects is the most objective and decisive
argument of all. I shall use the sign M as a convenient symbol
for the sayings and parables which are found only in Matthew.
With Streeter and Bussmann I believe that M was also a

[1] *Op. cit.*, 170.

[2] See the important essay of C. K. Barrett, 'Q: A Re-examination', ET vol.
liv, 320–3.

[3] *Einleitung in das Neue Testament* (1953), 162–82.

document, but it will not be possible within the limits of this essay to discuss this hypothesis, although the investigation will have something to contribute to it. It will not be necessary to examine the L hypothesis, and I must content myself with stating the belief that it was a body of oral tradition which Luke was the first to give a written form. All I wish to attempt is to consider whether the order of the sayings commonly assigned to Q is such as to render probable the view that this source lay before the two Evangelists in the form of a document at the time when they wrote.

In this endeavour I am compelled to refer to an article on 'The Order of Q' which I contributed to the *Journal of Theological Studies*[1] in April 1953, since the present essay carries further conclusions there suggested. In that article I made a new approach to the question of order by suggesting that we must not be content to study parallel passages in Matthew and Luke in two columns, with Luke on the left, as presumably representing better the original order of Q, and Matthew on the right. Such lists point to a common order, as many scholars have argued, but the breaches of order in the lists are so many that the case has been felt to be much less strong and convincing than, in fact, it is. In the article referred to I set down the Lukan passages on the left, but instead of one column for Matthew I used *six*, including the Q sayings in the five great discourses in Matthew, in 5-7, 10, 13, 18 and 23-25 and a sixth column containing the Q sayings in the rest of Matthew. The result was to show an astonishing range of agreement, not continuous throughout but visible in groups or series of passages in the same order in both Gospels. In all, only ten sayings stood apart from these series breaking their continuity, and it was suggested that, unless Luke used Matthew as a source, a strong argument existed in favour of the hypothesis that both Evangelists drew upon the document Q as one of their principal sources.

Obviously the tabulated series cannot be the result of happy chance, but, in default of any criticisms of the article known to me, I may perhaps be permitted to say that the table is open to two objections. First, I excluded a group of sayings and parables on the ground that in them by wide consent Matthew's

[1] Vol. IV, N.S., 27–31.

preference, while possibly using Q, is dependent upon another source, with the result that the order of Q, as reflected in Matthew and Luke, may be obscured.[1] Secondly, I did not discuss in detail the ten short sayings which stand in a different order in the two Gospels. The table was left to speak for itself.

In the present essay I shall include all the passages mentioned, with the exception of Matthew 16:2 which is textually suspect. The effect is to break to some extent the regularity of the agreements, although not in one or two cases, but in any case it makes the investigation more complete. I now propose to discuss the order of the Q sayings in Luke as compared with that present in the five great discourses in Matthew and in the rest of this Gospel outside these discourses.

[1] The passages omitted were the Great Commandment (Luke 10:25–8, Matthew 22:34–9), the Signs of the Times (Luke 12:54–6, Matthew 16:2f.), the Narrow Gate (Luke 13:23f., Matthew 7:13f.), the Shut Door (Luke 13:25–7, Matthew 25:10–12), the Great Supper (Luke 14:15–24, Matthew 22:1–10), the Lost Sheep (Luke 15:4–7, 10, Matthew 18:12–14), and the Pounds (Luke 19:12–27, Matthew 25:14–30).

II

THE SERMON ON THE MOUNT

Luke	Matthew 5–7
6:20–3	5:3–6, 11f.
6:27–30	5:39b–42
6:31	(7:12)
6:32–6	5:44–8
6:37f.	7:1f.
6:41f.	7:3–5
6:43–5	7:16–20
6:46	7:21
6:47–9	7:24–7
11:2–4	6:9–13
11:9–13	(7:7–11)
11:33	(5:15)
11:34	6:22f.
12:22–31	6:25–33
12:33b, 34	(6:20f.)
12:57–9	(5:25f.)
13:23f.	7:13f.
13:25–7	7:22f. [25:10–12]
14:34f.	(5:13)
16:13	(6:24)
16:17	5:18
16:18	5:32

Notes:

1. The greater part of Matthew's Version consists of sayings from M. In particular, 5:21–48 includes six 'Antitheses', together with an introduction in 5:17–20. Into these sections Q sayings have been inserted. It is not surprising, therefore, that in these cases Matthew and Luke do not agree in order.

2. Further, there is an original group of M sayings in 6:1–8, 16–18 (and perhaps also in 19–21). This also affects the order in which Q is used.

3. In these circumstances the agreement in the order of Q in the two Gospels is remarkable. The order is not continuous, but consists of sequences in common, of which the first (broken by 7:12) is considerable, and the second (broken by 7:7–11 and 5:15) is hardly less notable. Two briefer sequences, consisting of two sayings each, follow. The bracketed passages are those which differ in order.

4. It will be seen that Matthew has used practically the whole of Luke's Sermon on the Plain in Matthew 5 and 7, and in 6 various sayings from Luke 11–14 and 16. This distribution has the appearance of a consciously adopted plan.

5. The passages in brackets obviously call for special discussion, and it will be useful to consider first those in Matthew 5:17–48, and then those in the rest of the Matthaean Sermon.

The Q sayings in Matthew 5:17–48

The six Antitheses are (1) 21ff. on Murder, (2) 27ff. on Adultery, (3) 31f. on Divorce, (4) 33ff. on Vows and Oaths, (5) 38ff. on Retribution, and (6) 43ff. on Love of one's neighbour. The theme of the Introduction, 5:17–20, is the Attitude to be taken to the Law. Of the Q sayings in 5:17–48 that on reconciliation in 25f. is loosely appended to 24 in No. 1 and it is not surprising that the Lukan order is broken. What is surprising is that 18 (in the Introduction) and 32 in No. 3 stand in their Lukan order, and that the same is true of 39b–42 and 44–8 in Nos. 5 and 6. Nos. 2 and 4 contain no Q sayings.

These facts are naturally explained if Matthew has edited the Introduction and has himself added Nos. 3, 5, and 6 to an original group of three Antitheses in Nos. 1, 2, and 4. This hypothesis has independently been suggested by M. Albertz[1] and W. L. Knox[2] on literary grounds[3] and receives further support from the order of the Q sayings. With the exception of the editorial use of Matthew 5:25f., dependence on Q in Matthew 5:17–48 in an order common to Matthew and Luke is a reasonable assumption. Matthew 5:18 and 32 are used

[1] *Die synoptischen Streitgespräche* (1921), 146–9. The hypothesis is discussed in my *Formation of the Gospel Tradition* (1933), 97–9.

[2] *The Sources of the Synoptic Gospels*, II (1957), 19–25.

[3] T. W. Manson, *The Sayings of Jesus* (1949) [first published as Part II of *The Mission and Message of Jesus*, 1937], 162, suggests that the original arrangement was: introduction, 17 and 20, No. 1, 21f., No. 2, 27f., No. 3, 31f., No. 4, 33f., No. 5, 38f., No. 6, 43f., Conclusion, 48.

earlier than the parallel sayings in Luke because they are inserted by Matthew into this complex.

The Q Sayings in the Rest of the Sermon on the Mount

In their Lukan order these sayings are Matthew 7:12, 7:7–11, 5:15, 6:20f., 5:13, 6:24; and with these 7:13f. and 22f. may with advantage be considered.

(1) *Matthew* 7:12 (Luke 6:31): 'All things therefore whatsoever ye would that men should do unto you, even so do ye also unto them: for this is the law and the prophets.'

Apart from the Matthaean addition in the final clause, Matthew and Luke agree closely.[1] Dependence on Q is highly probable, and the only question to consider is why Matthew incorporates the saying at a later point. In reply, it is to be noted that both Evangelists use it as a summary passage. The position in Luke is much to be preferred since it is the conclusion to a group, Luke 6:27–30, arranged in Semitic parallelism and revealing both rhyme and rhythm when translated back into Aramaic.[2] Apparently, Matthew has delayed his use of the saying to sum up the considerable number of Q sayings in 6:22–7:11. In short, he alters Luke's order for editorial reasons.

(2) *Matthew* 7:7–11 (Luke 11:9–13): *On Answer to Prayer.*

The agreement is close, but the clue to the difference of position in the two Gospels is obscure. McNeile says that in Matthew the saying stands in no apparent relation to the context.[3] In Luke it appears in a section on Prayer (11:1–13) following the Lord's Prayer (2–4) and the parable of the Friend at Midnight (5–8). Knox[4] suggests that the section is a (pre-Lukan) tract on Prayer, but, if so, this suggestion does not exclude the probability that in Q Luke 11:9–13 originally followed immediately Luke 11:2–4. Why, then, in Matthew 7:7–11 is it separated from the Prayer (Matthew 6:9–13) by several passages from Q and M, placed immediately after the M saying, 'Give not that which is holy to the dogs', and before

---

[1] Dr. Manson *op. cit.*, 18f., suggests that 'whatsoever' (Matthew) and 'as' (Luke) may be alternative renderings of an Aramaic original, and that 'all things' and 'therefore' are probably editorial.

[2] Cf. Manson, *op. cit.*, 50; C. F. Burney, *The Poetry of our Lord*, 113, 169; M. Black, *An Aramaic Approach to the Gospels and Acts*, 137f.

[3] *The Gospel according to St. Matthew*, 91.

[4] *Op. cit.*, 60f.

the summary saying, 7:12, on doing to others as we wish them to do to us? No completely satisfactory answer has been given to this question, and it may be insoluble. Only a conjecture can be offered. The natural place for the passage in Matthew would be after the Lord's Prayer (Matthew 6:9–13) as in Luke. But at this point Matthew uses a saying from Mark or M on forgiveness (Matthew 6:14f.). This change of theme leaves the passage on Answer to Prayer on his hands; and he finds no place for it, save in an unsuitable context, after the extracts from Q and M immediately before 7:12 as indicated above. In any case and whatever may be the explanation, Matthew's use of 7:7–11 is probably editorial.

(3) *Matthew* 5:15 (Luke 11:33): 'Neither do men light a lamp, and put it under the bushel, but on the stand, and it shineth unto all that are in the house.'

Matthew 5:15 stands in an M context (Matthew 5:13–16) and may even belong to M. In this case no problem arises: Matthew follows the order of M. More probably, however, the saying has been taken from Q. The parallel passage in Luke 11:33 has a doublet in Luke 8:16 (=Mark 4:21) and shares with it the words οὐδείς, αψας, and εἰσπορευόμενοι and the idea that those who see the light enter from without. This explains the linguistic differences between Luke 11:33 and Matthew 5:15.[1] That a common source is used is suggested by the fact that Matthew 5:15, 6:22f., and 6:25–33 follow in the same relative order as Luke 11:33, 34f., and 12:22–31.[2] The earlier position of Matthew 5:15 is caused by its insertion in its present M context (see above).

(4) *Matthew* 6:20f. (Luke 12:33b–34): *Treasure on Earth and in Heaven.*

Apart from the closing words (Matthew 6:21 and Luke 12:34) the linguistic differences are considerable. These differences and the variation of rhythm[3] in the two forms suggest that Matthew is drawing upon M and Luke on Q. In this case the difference in position is not surprising.

---

[1] Matthew is probably nearer to the original in his use of the impersonal plural καίουσιν.

[2] It is noteworthy that if the differences of position of 7:7–11, 5:15, 6:20f., 5:25f. are editorial, the agreement in order extends from 6:9–13 to 7:22f.

[3] Cf. Burney, *op. cit.* 115.

(5) *Matthew* 5:13 (Luke 14:34f.) : *On Salt.*

Here again Matthew's source may be M.[1] If he is using Q the difference of order in Matthew and Luke is due to the M context in which Matthew 5:13 appears.

(6) *Matthew* 6:24 *On Serving Two Masters.*

The two versions are in almost verbatim agreement; the only difference is that Luke has οἰκέτης with οὐδείς. With the last saying this is one of those 'scattered fragments' which Streeter[2] says there is good reason to assign to Q, although they are not found embedded in the mass of other material from that source. Easton[3] soundly observes that its place in Q is quite uncertain.

It is possible to state a case in favour of the order of either of the Evangelists. Luke attaches it to a group of L sayings (Luke 16:10–12) which follow the parables of the Unjust Steward (16:1–9) and the connexion seems determined *ad vocem* by the word 'Mammon'. This arrangement appears to be artificial as compared with that of Matthew who uses the saying to introduce the passage on Anxiety (6:25–34). The two are connected by the phrase διὰ τοῦτο and the idea suggested is that, as we cannot serve two masters, we are not to be anxious for our life. This connexion is good, but somewhat artificial. Luke has the passage on Anxiety earlier (12:22–31) after the parable of the Rich Fool (12:13–21), and in this arrangement διὰ τοῦτο seems to point back to the preceeding Q saying on the guidance of the Holy Spirit in a time of anxiety (12:11f.). As in Matthew this connexion is good, but perhaps superficial. Anxiety about food and clothing and about one's defence before a legal tribunal are connected by little save the idea of anxiety itself. No compelling argument enables us to decide between Matthew and Luke and we must agree with the opinion of Easton, cited above, that the place of the saying on Serving Two Masters in Q is uncertain. Editorial activity has been at work in either Matthew or Luke, and perhaps in both.

(7) *Matthew* 7:13f. (Luke 13:23f.): The Two Ways, and Matthew 7:22f. (Luke 13:26f.): *The Shut Door.*

Linguistically the two sayings have so little in common that

---

[1] Cf. Manson, *op. cit.*, 132.
[2] *The Four Gospels*, 285–9.
[3] *The Gospel according to St. Luke*, 246.

it is possible that both have been taken from M.[1] Moreover, Matthew 7:13f. speaks of the narrow *gate* which leads to the ways of destruction and life, whereas Luke speaks of the narrow *door* which many are not able to enter. The sayings on the Shut Door also agree only in the common use of Psalm 6:9. Phrases in Luke 13:25 recall the parable of the Ten Virgins in M (Matthew 25:1–13).

The two sayings are considered here in order to have as many facts before us as possible because (a) they stand in the same order in Matthew and Luke, and (b) the intervening passages, Matthew 7:16–20 (Luke 6:43f.) and Matthew 7:21 (Luke 6:46), *also* stand in the same order.[2] Moreover, Matthew 7:16–20 and 21 also, like 7:13f. and 22f., may come from M. If the source is Q, Matthew has followed its order; if M, he (or the compiler of M) is aware of Q's order or of a tradition common to Q and M. Probably the editorial work is that of Matthew himself. He connects 7:16–20 and 21 because they stand in that order in the Lukan Sermon on the Plain (Q) and 7:13f. and 22f. because they follow in the same order in those passages outside of the Lukan Sermon which he uses in compiling the Sermon on the Mount.

Conclusions regarding the Sermon on the Mount

From the above investigation it would appear that, apart from cases of conflation with M, and insertions and additions to it, Matthew has followed the order of Q as it stood in Luke. The necessity of discussing cases where the order is broken must not obscure the fact that for the most part the agreement of order is patent and therefore does not need discussion. In the cases examined conflation and editorial changes are departures from the order present in Luke, except on rare occasions

[1] For this reason they were omitted with five other sayings in the JTS article mentioned at the outset (Group A).

[2] See the table on p. 98. The correspondences (with the Matthaean passages on the left) may be represented as follows:

Matthew	*Luke*	*Luke*
7:13f.		13:23f.
7:16–20	6:43f.	
7:21	6:46	
7:22f.		13:26f.

when Luke is responsible for the differences. A point of interest is that M supplies about two-thirds of the whole, which suggests that M itself contained a version of the Sermon beginning with Beatitudes. If so, Matthew has followed M in 5:3–11 with additions and modifications suggested by Q.

THE MISSION CHARGE

Luke	*Matthew* 9:37–10:42
6:40	(10:24f.)
10:2	9:37f.
10:3–12	10:9–16
10:16	(10:40)
12:2f.	10:26f.
12:4–7	10:28–31
12:8f.	10:32f.
12:11f.	(10:19f.)
12:51–3	10:34–6
14:26f.	10:37f.
17:33	10:39

Notes:

1. The Matthaean discourse contains material from M and Mark, but mainly from Q. (For 10:9–16 see footnote 2 below.)

2. It will be seen that, apart from 10:24f., 40, and 19f., the Q passages listed (24 verses) agree exactly in order in Matthew and Luke.

3. Obviously the three exceptions (5 verses) call for examination in order to see why they appear in a different order.

(1) *Matthew* 10:24f. (Luke 6:40): 'A disciple is not above his master, nor a servant above his lord' (Matthew); 'The disciple is not above his master: but every one when he is perfected shall be as his master' (Luke).

It should be noted that Luke 6:39 has a parallel in Matthew 14:14 which is also not in Luke's order. Luke 6:39f. is a unit, not connected closely with its context in the Lukan Sermon, which Matthew has not included in the Sermon on the Mount. In 15:14 he applies 39 to the Pharisees[1] and, as we see, sets 40 in the Mission Charge. Both Matthaean sayings stand in an M context and both may belong to M,[2] but the artificiality of the construction in 15:12–14 and 10:23–5 raises the question whether after all both have been derived from Q.

[1] This passage is considered later in the section headed 'The Rest of Matthew', p. 114f.

[2] Cf. Manson, *op. cit.* 57. Manson also suggests that Matthew 10:9–16 is a conflation of material from Mark, Q, and M, *op. cit.*, 180.

A common dependence on Q is suggested by the agreements and by the fact that Matthew's modifications appear to be secondary. Instead of the general application which the sayings have in Luke 6:39f. he applies 39 to the Pharisees and adapts 40 for use in the Mission Charge in 10:24f., where the context and the double use of the term 'his lord' suggest that he is thinking of Jesus Himself.

All this is true even if Luke 6:39f. is not in its original order. Creed[1] says that its position is editorial and Easton[2] thinks the connexion is artificial. But there is not a little to be said for the view that Luke retains the order of Q. Luke 6:39f. follows the saying on Not Judging (6:37f.) and precedes that on the Mote and the Beam (6:41f.). The idea appears to be that the man who condemns others is a blind guide who can benefit no one. Teacher and disciple alike will fall into a pit, for the disciple's insight will rise no higher than that of his teacher even if the lesson is learned perfectly. Moreover, the man who judges is blind in another sense. He sees the mote in his brother's eye, but not the beam in his own eye, and thus deceives himself. This connexion of thought seems too subtle to be editorial. It is easier to suppose that Luke is reproducing the order of Q.[3] If so, on his understanding of the sayings, Matthew has regarded them as unsuitable for the Sermon on the Mount and has transferred them to the contexts in which they now stand.

(2) *Matthew* 10:40 (Luke 10:16): 'He that receiveth you receiveth me, and he that receiveth me receiveth him that sent me' (Matthew); 'He that heareth you heareth me; and he that rejecteth you rejecteth me; and he that rejecteth me rejecteth him that sent me' (Luke). Cf. Mark 9:37, 'Whosoever shall receive one of such little children in my name, receiveth me: and whosoever receiveth me, receiveth not me, but him that sent me.'

It is important to note that, while these versions of the

---

[1] *The Gospel according to St. Luke*, 97.

[2] *Op. cit.*, 92.

[3] The opinion that 'He spake also a parable to them' (Luke 6:39) is editorial, is supported by Luke 5:36, 8:4, 12:16, 13:6, 14:7, 15:3, and 18:1; but Bussmann, *Synoptische Studien*, ii, 48, n.I, suggests that perhaps it is original and lost through Matthew's change of position. It may be a necessary connecting link in the sense of 'Take an illustration'.

saying are not in the same order in Matthew and Luke, each belongs to the conclusion of the Mission Charge in the two Gospels. Apparently, Matthew has postponed the use of it deliberately until he has used additional sayings from Q, M, and Mark. It is not certain, however, that Q is his source. Matthew 10:40f. may be from M and 10:42 is probably taken from Mark 9:41. Dr. Manson[1] says that Luke 10:16 is to be assigned to Q, but that one may have doubts whether Matthew 10:40 should be labelled Q or M. He further suggests that Matthew 10:40, Mark 9:37, and Luke 10:16 may go back to a fuller common original. The possibility arises that, if Matthew 10:40 is drawn from M, its position at the close of the Charge is suggested by the place of Luke 10:16. In any case, whether it be from Q or M, its use by Matthew is determined by editorial considerations.

(3) *Matthew* 10:19f. (Luke 12:11f.): 'But when they deliver you up, be not anxious *how* or *what* ye shall speak: for it shall be given you in that hour what ye shall speak. For it is not ye that speak, but the Spirit of your Father that speaketh in you' (Matthew); 'And when they bring you before the synagogues, and the rulers, and the authorities, be not anxious *how* or *what* ye shall answer, or what ye shall say: for the Holy Spirit shall teach you in that very hour what ye ought to say' (Luke). Cf. Mark 13:11 and Luke 21:14f.

The difference of order in Matthew and Luke is explained by the fact that the closer parallel to Matthew 10:19f. is Mark 13:11. Matthew's source in 10:17–22 is Mark 13:9–13. It is often maintained that Luke 12:11f. is from Q because of its small linguistic agreements with Matthew 10:19f. which are not present in Mark, especially the phrase 'how or what'. This view is weakened if, as Streeter thinks, the phrase is due to textual assimilation,[2] but it is not altogether destroyed. Streeter points out that in both Gospels the saying stands in the same discourse as Luke 12:2ff. =Matthew 10:26ff., though separated by a few verses, and argues that the presence of Luke 12:11f. explains the use of the saying in both Gospels.[3] Q may have suggested to Matthew the use of Mark 13:9–13 in

[1] *Op. cit.*, 78, 183.
[2] *Op. cit.*, 280.
[3] *Ibid.*

the Mission Charge rather than in the Eschatological discourse in Matthew 24 where it is merely summarized (Matthew 24:9, 13).

Conclusions regarding the Mission Charge

In considering the above passages one must not forget that, even more impressively than in the Sermon on the Mount, much the greater number of Q sayings (approximately four-fifths) are in the same order in Matthew and Luke. Where there is a difference of order, the arrangement in Matthew (and possibly occasionally in Luke) is due to editorial reasons or the use of other sources and that in some cases (10:19f. and 40) Matthew appears to be aware of the order he deserts. Thus, the differences do not weaken the hypothesis of a common order, but tend to confirm it.

THE DISCOURSE ON TEACHING IN PARABLES

In this, the third of Matthew's five discourses, most of the material is taken from the two sources, Mark (4:1–9, 10–12, 13–20, 30–2) and M (Matthew 13:24–30, 36–43, 44, 45f., 47–50, 51f.). The Q material is limited to one saying and two parables (The Mustard Seed and the Leaven), of which the Mustard Seed (Matthew 13:31f.) is a conflation of the Q version with Mark 14:30–2.[1] This material, arranged in the Lukan order, is as follows:

Luke	*Matthew*	
10:23f.	13:16f.	'Blessed are the eyes which see.'
13:18f.	13:31f.	The Mustard Seed.
13:20f.	13:33	The Leaven.

Notes:

1. There are no Q passages in an order other than that of Luke.

2. It is reasonable to suppose that in constructing the discourse Matthew takes his point of departure from Mark 4:1, adding a considerable amount of parabolic matter from M, and inserting extracts from Q.

3. He conflates the Q version of the Mustard Seed (Luke 13:18f.) with Mark 4:30–2, and appends the parables of the Leaven because the two stood together in Q.

4. Already Matthew has on his hands the saying, 'Blessed are your eyes' (Luke 10:23f.=Matthew 13:16f.), having replaced this passage by the M saying, 'Come unto me, all ye that labour' (Matthew 11:28–30), after the saying, 'I thank thee, O Father, Lord of heaven and earth' (Luke 10:21f.=Matthew 11:25–7).

[1] Cf. Streeter, *op. cit.*, 246–8.

He places the saying after the Markan passage on the Purpose of Parables (Mark 4:10–12=Matthew 13:10–15), adding the phrase 'and your ears, for they hear' and substituting 'righteous men' for 'kings'. As Easton[1] says, the arrangement is obviously artificial. Matthew chooses the best place he can find for the saying previous to the second and third extracts from Q fixed by the use of Mark 4:30–2, the parable of the Mustard Seed.

5. It is to be noted that Matthew had already used all the Q material in Luke which stands before 11:23f., as well as all the sayings between this passage and the parable of the Mustard Seed (Luke 13:18f.), with the exception of the saying on the Great Commandment (Luke 10:25–28). Thus, the three extracts from Q stood together ready for use in Matthew 13.

Conclusions on the Discourse on Teaching in Parables

The amount of Q sayings in the discourse is small, but, so far as it goes, it confirms the hypothesis that Matthew follows the order of Q as it is reflected in Luke.

THE DISCOURSE ON DISCIPLESHIP

The fourth Matthaean discourse is constructed like the third. It consists of material taken almost wholly from Mark (9:33–7, 42–8) in 18:1–9 and from M in 18:10–35. A few Q sayings appear to be used in the order in which they are found in Luke.

Luke	Matthew	
14:11	18:4	On humbling oneself.
[15:4–7, 10]	[18:12–14]	The Lost Sheep.
17:1f.	18:6f.	On Stumbling-blocks.
17:3f.	18:15, 21	On Forgiveness.

The extent to which Matthew uses Q in these passages is debatable.

It is open to question if the second belongs to Q. Matthew 18:4 differs considerably from Luke 14:11, and Matthew 18:6f. and 15, 21 are conflations of material from Q dna M.

All the more remarkable is the agreement in order shown above. Moreover, Matthew had not to search for the Q sayings: they probably lay immediately before the eye He had already drawn upon all the sayings in Q which precede Luke 14:11 and those also which lie between this saying and Luke 17:1, which, with the exception of the sayings listed above, stood in succession ready for use in 18.

[1] *Op. cit.*, 168.

In view of the difficult questions which arise in these sayings it is necessary to examine them in detail.

(1) *Matthew* 18:4 (Luke 14:11): 'Whosoever therefore shall humble himself *as this* little child, the same is the greatest in the kingdom of heaven' (Matthew); 'For every one that exalteth himself shall be humbled; and he that humbleth himself shall be exalted' (Luke). Cf. Luke 18:14b and Matthew 23:12, which are in almost verbatim agreement with Luke 14:11.

Luke 14:11 is attached loosely to the section on Table Manners (14:7–10) and similarly the doublet in Luke 18:14b is a pendant to the parable of the Pharisee and the Tax-gatherer (18:9–14a). Matthew 23:12 stands at the end of an M section which condemns the habit of seeking respect from others, and Matthew 18:4, which is the passage under review, in an insertion in the story derived from Mark 9:33–7 on True Greatness.

Many scholars describe the passage as 'a floating saying'[1] or as 'a short proverbial saying' for which there is no need to postulate a written source at all.[2]

On the whole it seems best to assign Luke 14:11 =Matthew 18:4 to Q and to explain Luke 18:14b and Matthew 23:12 as repetitions of the saying. Hesitation to take this view is natural, for at first sight Matthew 18:4 seems widely different from Luke 14:11. But the differences, underlined above, are modifications due to the Markan context in which it appears (cf. Mark 9:34, 36). Thus, Matthew 18:4 is more than 'a reminiscence of Q'[3]; it is a conscious modification of Q for editorial reasons.

(2) *Matthew* 18:12–14 (Luke 15:4–7, 10): The Lost Sheep. This parable is widely assigned to Q,[4] but the opinion of Streeter,[5] endorsed by T. W. Manson,[6] that Matthew's version belongs to M and Luke's to L, is highly probable. The

---

[1] Cf. Manson, *op. cit.*, 312.

[2] Cf. Streeter, *op. cit.*, 285.

[3] Easton, *op. cit.*, 227.

[4] Cf. Bussmann, *op. cit.*, II, 86f.; Easton, *op. cit.*, xix, 235f. Creed, *op. cit.*, lxv; G. D. Kilpatrick, *The Origins of the Gospel according to St. Matthew*, 28f.; S. E. Johnson, *The Interpreter's Bible*, vii, 471.

[5] *Op. cit.*, 244f.

[6] *Op. cit.*, 283.

words common to both are those without which the story could not be told, and where the versions can differ, they do. Some of the differences are apparently translation variants.[1] The setting and the moral of the two versions are also different. In Matthew the parable is set in an M context and is related to the despising of 'little ones'; in Luke it precedes two other similar parables from L (the Lost Coin and the Lost Son) and its theme is the mercy of God in forgiving sinners. An inordinate amount of editorial modification has to be assigned to Luke if both versions are drawn from a common source, whereas the differences are intelligible if they come from different cycles of tradition.

If this view is taken, the variation in order is irrelevant. Just because this fact is consistent with the main contentions of this essay it is necessary to consider what follows if the common source is Q. In this case the different order is the result of editorial adjustments with the other sources mentioned above on the part of one or both of the Evangelists.

(3) *Matthew* 18:6f. (Luke 17:1f.); On Offences.

Matthew's version is widely held to be a conflation of Mark and Q, a view which accounts for the reverse form in which the saying appears in Matthew and Luke.[2]

(4) *Matthew* 18:15, 21f. (Luke 17:3f.): On Forgiveness.

The verbal agreements are slight, and from these it is impossible to maintain that the two versions are derived from one common source. Moreover, the number of the acts of forgiveness differs (Matthew seventy times seven, or seventy-seven; Luke, seven times), and 'I repent' is peculiar to Luke. But there is agreement in the succession of themes (Offences and Forgiveness).[3] The presumption is that Matthew is giving the fuller M version in 18:15–22 in preference to that of Q for liturgical reasons.

Conclusions regarding the Discourse on Discipleship

Although the Q sayings used or reflected in the discourse

[1] Cf. Manson, *op. cit.*, 208, J. Jeremias, *The Parables of Jesus*, 29, 106.

[2] Cf. Streeter, *op. cit.*, 265, 281 n.; Easton, *op. cit.*, 256; Creed, *op. cit.*, 214; Klostermann, *Das Lukasevangelium*, 170.

[3] Cf. Streeter, *op. cit.*, 281, 'Seeing there is no very obvious connection between the two topics, the connection (Offences-Forgiveness) must have been made in the common source Q'.

are few, they follow without exception the Lukan order. It is possible that order of thought in Q, humility, offences, and forgiveness, is the clue to Matthew's disposal of Markan and M material in 18:1–9 (Mark) and 10–35 (M).

THE ESCHATOLOGICAL DISCOURSE

Whether Matthew 23 (the Condemnation of the Scribes and Pharisees) should be separated from the Eschatological Discourse proper in Matthew 24–5 is a disputed question. Certainly 23 is self-contained, but it is not concluded by the formula, 'And it came to pass, when Jesus had finished all these words', which appears at the end of the five great discourses (cf. 26:1). It appears to be Matthew's intention to connect 23 with 24–5 (cf. 23:38). Since, however, it forms a whole, it will be useful to examine it separately.

Luke	Matthew
11:39–48	23:4–31
11:19–51	23:34–6
11:52	(23:13)
13:34f.	23:37–9

Notes:

1. It will be seen that there is a relative agreement of order broken, apparently, at Matthew 23:13.

2. The table, however, is delusive unless we consider Matthew 23:4–31 (to which verse 13 belongs) in detail, since M forms the backbond of this section, Mark 12:38b–40 is inserted in 23:6–7a and 13(f) almost verbatim. Several of the parallels in Luke 11, which presumably are from Q, are slight and not in the Lukan order. In these circumstances it will be helpful to set out the whole of Matthew 23 in a table indicating the parallel sayings in Luke and the extent to which they agree linguistically.

In their Matthaean order the parallel sayings are as follows:

Matthew 23	Luke	Agreement
1		
2f.		
4	11:46	Small
5		
6–7a	11:43	Small
7b–10		
11		
12	(cf. 14:11)	Almost verbatim

(*Continued*)

Matthew 23	Luke	Agreement
13f.	11:32	Small
15–22		
23:23	11:42	Considerable
24		
25f.	11:39–41	Considerable
27f.	11:44	Negligible
29–31	11:47f.	Small
32f.		
34–6	11:49–51	Considerable
37–9	13:34f.	Almost verbatim

Note:
The horizontal lines separate the seven 'Woes' in Matthew from the rest of the chapter.

From this table it can be seen that the first five parallels stand in a different order in Matthew and Luke. They appear to be cases in which a definite preference has been given to the order and text of M. Only Matthew 23:12 is a probable insertion from Q and 23:23 may be a conflation of Q and M. In these circumstances the difference or order in the five parallels is not in the least surprising.

All the more remarkable is the complete agreement of order in the last five parallels. Moreover, apart from Matthew 23:27f. and 29–31 the linguistic agreement is much greater. Apparently in these two sayings Matthew is still dependent on M. The agreement in order might be accidental or due to the original tradition lying behind M and Q, but the considerable degree of linguistic agreement of 23:25f., 34–6, and 37–9[1] with their Lukan counterparts suggests rather a knowledge of the order of the five sayings in Q, and 23:23 may well have drawn Matthew's attention to this series.

We must conclude that, although Matthew follows M in the main in 23, he is well aware of the order of Q and observes it in the latter part of the discourse.

Matthew 24–25.

In the Eschatological Discourse proper the parallel passages in their Lukan order are:

[1] Dr. Manson, *op. cit.*, 102, points out that, taking Luke's shorter version as the standard, the amount of agreement in Matthew 23:34f. it is near 90 per cent.

Luke	Matthew
12:39f.	24:43f.
12:42–6	24:45–51
17:23f.	24:26f.
17:26f.	24:37–9
17:34f.	24:40f.
17:37	(24:28)
19:12–27	25:14–30

Notes:

1. There are two parallel series, the second of which is broken by Matthew 24:28 (the Gathering Vultures).

2. The questions to be discussed are why 24:43–51 (the Parables of the Thief and the Faithful and Unfaithful Servants) appears later in Matthew, and why 24:28 is used earlier than in Luke.

(1) *Matthew* 24:43–51. The first question is easily answered. The two parables are attached to the Markan saying (13:35) in Matthew 24:42 to form the first and second of a group of five parables (the last three of which, the Ten Virgins, the Talents,[1] and the Sheep and the Goats, are from M) in Matthew 24:43–25; 46 (i.e. at the end of the Discourse).

(2) *Matthew* 24;28: 'Wheresoever the carcase is, there will be the vultures gathered together' (Matthew), 'And they answering say unto him, Where, Lord? And he said unto them, Where the body is, thither will the vultures also be gathered together' (Luke).

In Matthew, without an opening question, it stands in a good connexion after the saying on the suddenness of the Coming of the Son of Man; in Luke it closes the Eschatological Discourse. In Matthew it affirms the inevitability of the Parousia; in Luke it amounts to a refusal to answer the question, 'Where, Lord?' Commentators are very divided on the question of its original position, and this is not strange since the saying is a proverbial utterance. The roughness of Luke's enigmatic form may be more original than Matthew's smoother version, but a certain decision is perhaps not possible. In any case the editorial activity of one or other of the Evangelists is responsible for the difference of position.

Conclusions regarding the Eschatological Discourse

As in 23, Matthew has used material from M and Mark with which he has connected extracts from Q. In the latter Matthew

---

[1] The parable of the Talents (in Luke the Pounds) appears to be a conflation of M and Q (cf. Matthew 25:24–9 and Luke 19:20–6).

and Luke agree in order apart from editorial rearrangements in Matthew 24:43–51 due to use of M, and perhaps also in 24:28 where Q alone is in question.

In all the five discourses we meet with the same features—respect in the main for the order of Q as it appears in Luke and editorial activity usually on the part of Matthew where the order is different. It remains now to ask if the same is true of the use of Q in the rest of Matthew outside the five great discourses.

THE REST OF MATTHEW

The Q passages in the Lukan order are as follows:

Luke	Matthew
3:7–9, 12, 16f.	3:7–12
3:21f.	3:16f.
4:1–13	4:1–11
6:39	(15:14)
6:43–5	(12:33–5)
7:1–10	8:5–10, 13
7:18–23	11:2–6
7:24–8	11:7–11
7:31–5	11:16–19
9:57–60	(8:19–22)
10:13–15	11:21–3
10:21f.	11:25–7
10:25–7	(22:34–9)
11:14–23	12:22–30
11:24–26	12:43–5
11:29–32	12:38–42
12:10	(12:32)
13:28f.	(8:11f.)
13:30	(20:16)
14:15–24	[22:1–10]
16:16	(11:12f.)
17:5f.	17:20
22:28, 30b	19:28

Notes:

1. It is a remarkable fact that, with the exception of the passages in brackets and the inversion of Matthew 12:43–5 and 38–42, all the sayings stand in the same order in Matthew and Luke.

2. The passage in square brackets is the parable of the Marriage Feast (Matthew 22:1–10, Luke 14:15–24, the Great Supper). It is included for the sake of completeness. Linguistically Matthew and Luke have very little in common and conflation in Matthew of Q with another parable is a probable explanation.[1]

3. Of the remaining passages in brackets Matthew 12:32 (cf. Mark 3:28f.) and

[1] Cf. Manson, *op. cit.*, 129, 225.

22:34–9 (cf. Mark 12:28–34) are conflations of Q and Mark which, as many examples have shown, result in a difference of order.

4. The passages left for discussion are Matthew 15:14, 12:33–5, 8:19–22, 8:11f., 20:16, and 11:12f.

The inversion of Matthew 12:43–7, 38–42 *and Luke* 11:24–6, 29–32

Editorial rearrangement is the cause of the inversion. In Matthew the sections on the Sign of Jonah and the Ninevites are brought together because they relate to Jonah, and the addition, 'Even so shall it be also unto this generation', brings the saying on Demon Possession (12:43–5) into harmony with the whole. In Luke the saying on Demon Possession stands first after the section on Collusion with Beelzebub, presumably because both deal with exorcism. Opinions will differ regarding the original order of Q. Matthew, I think, is responsible for the inversion, but in either case a common order is presupposed.

(1) *Matthew* 15:14 (Luke 6:39): 'Let them alone: they are blind guides. And if the blind guide the blind, both shall fall into a pit' (Matthew); 'And he spoke also a parable unto them, Can the blind guide the blind? shall they not both fall into a pit?' (Luke).

It will be recalled that the saying which follows (Luke 6:40 =Matthew 10:24f.) was discussed earlier, and that the view taken was that Luke 6:39f. preserves the order of Q, Matthew 10:24f. owing its position to the M context in which it stands. A similar explanation accounts for the position of Matthew 15:14 which reflects editorial rearrangement.[1]

(2) *Matthew* 12:33–5 (Good and Corrupt Trees); cf. Matthew 7:16–20 and Luke 6:43–5 discussed earlier.

The relationships between Matthew 7:16–20 and 12:33–5 are difficult to determine. Easton[2] suggests different forms in which the saying was spoken. With greater probability Hawkins[3] suggests that Matthew uses the saying twice, adapting it to the context in which he places it, in 7:16–18 to bring out the criterion of true and false teachers, in 12:33–5 to bring out the importance of words as proofs of the state of

---

[1] Cf. Manson, *op. cit.*, 57.

[2] *Op. cit.*, 92.

[3] *Horae Synopticae*, 85.

men's hearts.[1] If this is so, editorial activity accounts for the fact that 12:33–5 is not in the Lukan order.

(3) *Matthew* 8:19–22 (Candidates for Discipleship); cf. Luke 9:57–60.

Why does Matthew place these sayings at an earlier point than that of Luke? Easton[2] gives the answer when he says that in both Matthew and Luke this is the last discourse section before the Mission Charge. *After* the Charge Matthew places those relating to the Baptist (11:2–6, 7–11, 16–19), while Luke has the parallel sayings *before* it (7:18–23, 24–8, 31–5). Further, Matthew has used 8:19–22 as a preface to a considerable group from Mark and M containing many miracle-stories. The purpose of this arrangement is to prepare the way for 11:5f. (Luke 7:22f.), which is the message to John about the mighty works being wrought by Jesus. Luke meets the same need by the editorial passage, 7:21, 'In that hour he cured many of diseases and plagues and evil spirits; and on many that were blind he bestowed sight.' Both Evangelists exercise editorial freedom, but in Matthew the order of Q is affected.

(4) *Matthew* 8:11f. (Luke 13:28f.): 'Many shall come from the east and the west . . .'

Matthew has used the saying earlier by inserting it into the story of the Centurion's Servant (8:5–10, 13) and has inverted the sentences in order to get a better connexion.

(5) *Matthew* 20:16 (Luke 13:30) (the Last First and the First Last).

The transposition of No. 4 (above) left the saying[3] isolated and Matthew has attached it to the parable of the Labourers in the Vineyard (20:1–15).

(6) *Matthew* 11:12f. (Luke 16:16): 'From the days of John the Baptist.'

In the interests of a better order Matthew has transferred the saying to an earlier point after the testimony of Jesus to

---

[1] Cf. Manson, *op. cit.*, 59, 'It is difficult to resist the conclusion that the Q material given here (Luke 6:43–5) in Luke has been freely adapted in Matthew to other purposes.'

[2] *Op. cit.*, 155.

[3] The source of the doublet in Matthew 19:30 is Mark 10:31 where, as in Matthew, the clauses are inverted (the First Last and the Last First).

John (11:7–11). Luke would hardly have moved it from this position if Q had so placed it.[1]

Conclusions regarding the Rest of Matthew

The use of Q in its Lukan order is as pronounced as in any of the five great discourses. It may be conjectured that, if the discourses were constructed first, the Q sayings were left standing as they appear in Luke. The changes of order are editorial or due to conflation with Mark. They arise from the necessity of inserting the sayings in the Markan framework and the desire to bring together and to adjust those relating to the Baptist.

III

CONCLUSIONS REGARDING Q AS A WHOLE

The investigation has confirmed the view that Luke has preserved the order of Q and has followed it with great fidelity. It has shown further that Matthew knew the same order and was aware of it when he made editorial adjustments and conflated Q with Mark and M. If we reject, as we must, the hypothesis of Luke's dependence on Matthew, the result of a comparison of the order of the sayings in Matthew and Luke is to demonstrate the existence of Q, so far as this is possible in the case of a source known to us only from its use in the two Gospels. Q is not 'an unnecessary and vicious hypothesis', but a collection of sayings and parables which actually existed when Matthew and Luke wrote. Its earlier history is a matter for conjecture; it is not excluded that earlier groups of sayings and parables have been combined in it. But this stage was past when the Gospels were compiled, and what we are able to recover is the form in which Q was current at least as early as the decade A.D. 50–60 and perhaps even earlier. It is probable that some of the sayings peculiar to Luke belong to it, including 6:24–6, 9:61f., 12:35–8, 47f., and 54–6, but not sayings found only in Matthew.

[1] Cf. Streeter, *Oxford Studies in the Synoptic Problem* (ed. W. Sanday), 156f.

It is desirable that M should be investigated more closely. This task has been waiting for a generation,[1] and it will always prove difficult, since the sayings are found in Matthew only.

(1959)

---

[1] An important contribution has been made by Professor Pierson Parker in *The Gospel before Mark* (1953), who has shown that 'since Q has not been assimilated to Matthaean types of expression', and 'the style of Q does not pervade M, therefore Q and M have different origins' and that 'Q is really from an autonomous source' (p. 30f.).

IX

The 'Son of Man' Sayings relating to
the Parousia

I

IN THIS ARTICLE I desire to set out a hypothesis to which sufficient attention has not been given. I do not necessarily accept it myself, but I present it because I think that progress in solving a very difficult critical problem may be secured by discussing it. Broadly stated, the hypothesis is that the 'Son of Man' sayings relating to the Parousia belong to the *earlier* part of the Ministry of Jesus and represent a stage which was subsequently passed in His thought and teaching.

As is well known, these sayings stand, in the main, in the later chapters of the Gospels, where they describe a Parousia which has yet to be fulfilled; they voice the eschatological hope not only of primitive Christianity, but of Jesus Himself. This representation raises the most serious difficulties, and all the more in view of the growing importance which modern criticism is attaching to the 'Son of Man' sayings relating to the Passion. If it be true, as I have no doubt it is, that Jesus reinterpreted the idea of the Son of Man in terms of the doctrine of the Suffering Servant of the Lord, is it not strange that concurrently and subsequently He should have uttered other sayings about the Son of Man which lack this original note and, on the contrary, are more closely in line with conventional Jewish expectations? It has been commonly held that these sayings express His confidence of triumph over suffering and death. There is much force in this contention, but it is subject to two disabilities. First, as thus understood, these sayings are doublets of His prophecies of resurrection, and it is not easy to harmonize the two. Secondly, it is just in these 'Son of Man' sayings relating to the Parousia that the impression is received that Jesus is speaking of someone or something

other than Himself. By the coming of the Son of Man in glory
with the angels of God does He mean Himself? It is, I think,
reasonably clear that if the chronological order were: (1) Son
of Man sayings relating to the Parousia, and (2) Son of Man
sayings with reference to suffering, we should have the basis
for an intelligible order of development in describing the life
and teaching of Jesus. The history of criticism, however,
supplies many warnings against premature attempts to sketch
the career of Jesus, which ought to put us on our guard against
doctrinaire methods. The fundamental appeal is to the
evidence.

The Synoptic evidence is striking. If we collect all the sayings
concerning the Son of Man which have an eschatological
setting, placing in brackets those which for various reasons are
of doubtful historical value, the list is as follows: Mark (8:38;)
13:26; 14:62; Luke 12:40; 17:22, 24, 26, 30; 18:8b; 21:36;
22:69; Matthew 10:23; (13:37, 41) (19:28) 24:27, (30), 37,
39, 44; (25:31f.).

Some comment on the bracketed sayings is clearly necessary.
Mark 8:38, which speaks of the coming of the Son of Man 'in
the glory of his Father with the holy angels,' is open to objection
because the parallel saying in Q, Luke 12:8f. = Matthew 10:32,
while eschatological, lacks this reference to the Parousia.
Matthew 13:37 and 41 belong to the exposition of the Parable
of the Tares. We should be on uncertain ground in using
Matthew 19:28 ('in the regeneration when the Son of Man
shall sit on the throne of his glory') because the parallel saying
on 'Thrones' in Luke 22:30 lacks the passage quoted, and in
any case does not assert, though it may imply, the Coming of
the Son of Man. Matthew 24:30 and 25:31f. are coloured by
imagery from the Similitudes of Enoch, and it is difficult to
decide how far they preserve the *ipsissima verba* of Jesus.
Without wishing to imply that the last word has been said
about Mark 8:38, Matthew 19:28; 24:30, and 25:31f., we
shall do well to set these sayings aside for our immediate
purpose.

It may occasion surprise that Matthew 10:23: 'Ye shall not
have gone through the cities of Israel, till the Son of man be
come,' is not included in the list of doubtful sayings. It is
possible, however, that in summarily rejecting the authenticity

of this saying modern criticism has been influenced too much by the use made of it in Schweitzer's theory, and has acquiesced too readily in the view that it reflects the historical situation when Matthew wrote, with the result that valuable evidence is lost for the purposes of historical reconstruction.

Turning to the sayings in the list which remain, we find that most of them appear in the Apocalyptic Discourses of Mark 13, and Luke 17, or are appended thereto in Matthew or Luke. If such passages are underlined the list is as follows: Mark 13:26; 14:62; Luke 12:40; 17:22, 24, 26, 30; 18:8b; 21:36; 22:69; Matthew 10:23; 24:27, 37, (39), 44. If, further, we arrange the sayings according to the sources, Mark, Q, M, and L, the results are more suggestive still:

Mark : 13:26; 14:62 (=? Luke 22:69).

Q : Luke 17:24 = Matthew 24:27.
Luke 17:26 = Matthew 24:37(39).
Luke 12:40 = Matthew 24:44.

M : Matthew 10:23.

L : Luke 17:22 (?Q).
Luke 17:30 (?Q).
Luke 18:8b.
Luke 21:36.

All the Matthæan passages are determined, in context, by Mark 13, and the same is true also of Luke 21:36 as this saying is commonly explained. *The Apocalyptic Document embedded in Mark 13 is a lodestone which has attracted to itself the majority of the sayings about the Coming of the Son of Man.* A parallel process can be seen in the Apocalyptic Discourse in Q (Luke 17). If, moreover, as I think, a third Apocalyptic Discourse is the basis of Luke 21, this also has drawn to itself Mark 13:26 in Luke 21:27. In short, all the sayings which speak of the Parousia of the Son of Man, except Mark 14:62, Matthew 10:23, Luke 12:40, and 18:8b, stand in Apocalyptic Discourses. This fact is highly significant; for it is certain that all these discourses are artificial compilations. The presence in them of the sayings in question gives us no assurance that they belong to the period shortly before the Passion. They can have been uttered *at any point* in the Historic Ministry.

But this is not all. Of the four remaining sayings only two, Mark 14:62 and Matthew 10:23, are connected with a definite historical situation, the former with the Trial before Caiaphas, the latter with the Mission Charge to the Twelve. These Sayings will call for further consideration. The other sayings, Luke 12:40 and Luke 18:8b, are attached to Parables. Luke 12:40, 'For in an hour that ye think not the Son of man cometh,' is the climax to the Parable of the Thief at Midnight. It may have been current as an isolated saying (cf. Easton, *St. Luke*, 206), but even if it belongs to the Parable, we do not know when it was spoken. Matthew (24:42–4) inserts this Parable into the framework supplied by the Apocalyptic Discourse of Mark 13. Luke 18:8b, 'Howbeit when the Son of man cometh, shall he find faith on the earth?', is loosely appended to the Parable of the Unjust Judge. It 'strikes a different note from the urgency of the preceding parable' (Creed), and it is explained as a redactional supplement by Bultmann, Klostermann, and other commentators. Accordingly, from the investigation as a whole, we reach the conclusion that, *with the exception of Mark 14:62 and Matthew 10:23, no 'Son of Man' saying relative to the Parousia need be assigned to the last stages of the Ministry, but may equally well belong to any stage, even the earliest.* To this conclusion the exception, Mark 14:62 which stands at the end, and Matthew 10:23 which may belong to the middle period, are of such interest and importance as to demand separate and fuller consideration.

II

Mark 14:62 and its Synoptic parallels read as follows:

Mark 14:62:   'I am: and ye shall see the Son of man sitting at the right hand of power, and coming with the clouds of heaven.'

Matthew 26:64: 'Thou hast said: nevertheless I say unto you, Henceforth (ἀπ' ἄρτι) ye shall see the Son of man sitting at the right hand of power, and coming on the clouds of heaven.'

Luke 22:69:   'But from henceforth (ἀπὸ τοῦ νῦν) shall
the Son of man be seated at the right hand
of the power of God.'

The agreement of Matthew and Luke in describing a
state which will obtain 'henceforth' raises the possibility that
a parallel phrase also stood originally in Mark, where it is read
by sy[8] (cf. Glasson, *The Second Advent*, 65–8); but, in any case,
this independent agreement implies that so the saying was
interpreted in the earliest times. Moreover, if Luke 22:69
belongs to a Passion Narrative independent of Mark, we have
primitive testimony to a text which did not speak of a coming
with the clouds, but of the triumphant session of the Son of
Man on high at the right hand of God. Even, however, if we
accept the Markan version of the saying, it by no means follows
that Jesus promised to Caiaphas a *spectacular* return of the
Son of Man to earth. Doubtless it was in this sense that the
Early Church interpreted the saying, and probably Mark
himself read it so (cf. 8:38; 13:26). By such an interpretation the
Apocalyptic hope of the first Christians was fed, and in
consequence of it, we may infer, the Son of Man sayings
relating to the Parousia were collected and placed in the
Apocalyptic Discourses of Mark 13, Matthew 24, Luke 17,
and 21, in which they now appear. But what did Jesus Himself
mean by His words to Caiaphas?

We shall be on surer ground if we begin, not with the
exegesis of Daniel 7:13, but with the historical circumstances in
which Jesus stood before the High Priest. There death stared
Him in the face, and with it, judged by every human standpoint,
the ruin of His hopes for the Kingdom and the final disproof
of His claim to be the Son of Man. Nevertheless, in that tragic
hour Jesus refuses to despair. To the question: 'Art thou the
Christ, the Son of the Blessed?', He answers with a confident
'I am,' or, if with early MSS. we read σὺ εἶπας ὅτι ἐγώ εἰμι
(Θ fam. 13 47² 543 565 700 1071 geo arm Or), 'Thou hast
said it thyself.' Not content, however, with an affirmation, He
boldly declares that the two Old Testament prophecies, Psalm
110:1 and Daniel 7:13, will be manifestly and speedily fulfilled.
We have no right to infer that ὄψεσθε necessarily implies a
spectacle visible to the eye (cf. Deuteronomy 28:10, Psalm 49:10,

Psalm 89:48); it can refer to what will be perceived in the order of God's working. And, if we have to choose which of these alternatives is most accordant with the mind of Jesus as we find it revealed in the Gospels, and especially when He interprets the Old Testament, there can be no doubt where our preference must lie. Dr. Glasson has done us a service in reminding us that the vision of Daniel 7 does not describe a descent to earth, but the coming with clouds of one 'like unto a son of man' to the Ancient of Days to receive dominion and glory *and a kingdom.* We do not need to think of Jesus, like a modern commentator, penetrating to the original meaning of Daniel. We have rather to confess that, under eschatological presuppositions, we ourselves have misread Daniel, and that his plain meaning was visible to the eyes of Jesus. What He means, in addressing Caiaphas, is that, despite appearances, He is not self-deceived; He will be glorified and the Kingdom will come. This interpretation does not imply that the real basis of the Advent Hope is mistaken, and that, in some way unknown to us, Jesus will not make Himself known to His own; it does mean that what the Early Church believed, and what the disposal of the Parousia sayings in the Gospels suggests, are perversions of His confident prophecy of Messianic triumph.

In turning to Matthew 10:23, 'Ye shall not have gone through the cities of Israel, till the Son of man be come,' we face a different and more difficult problem. In recoil from Schweitzer's use of this saying, modern criticism has settled down to the conviction that the saying represents the ideas of the Early Church rather than the words of Jesus, and that it was formed in the stress of controversy between St. Paul and the Church of Jerusalem. It may be that the time has come to revise this interpretation, and that, in accepting it too readily and without qualification, we have lost the key without which the Son of Man sayings remain an insoluble problem; in short, that we have destroyed important evidence.

The view maintained by Streeter, Manson, C. J. Cadoux, and other scholars that Matthew 10:23 echoes the controversy between the Jewish-Christian and Gentile-Christian sections of the Primitive Church, and was perhaps modified thereby, need not be questioned. In compiling the Mission Charge to the Twelve from Mark, Q, and M, Matthew cannot have been

unmindful of existing conditions and those which had obtained
in the preceding decades; and we need not doubt that Matthew
10:23 was quoted and re-quoted in the Gentile controversy.
If so, the saying must have been current in the period *c.* A.D. 50,
and is probably much older. Used in controversy it must have
been reinterpreted: Jesus had promised that the Son of Man
would come before the cities of Israel were evangelized; wherein
lay the justification for the Gentile Mission? So Jewish-
Christians may have argued during the Council of Jerusalem!
Reinterpretation, however, is one thing; invention another.
A saying unfulfilled in the experience of the Twelve to whom it
was first spoken might be given a new meaning in the light of a
later day. But would it have been *invented* for this purpose? It
is one thing to overcome an embarrassment left by an unfulfilled
prophecy, quite another thing to create historical difficulties
by inventing an assurance to the Twelve at variance with fact.
The presumption is that not only is the saying early but that
it is original, and that it has survived only because it was given
a new application.

III

To what conclusions does the evidence, as discussed above,
point? A decisive answer is not possible, but the following
inferences deserve consideration.

(1) The evidence which has been used to connect the
Parousia sayings with the closing days of the Ministry is very
uncertain. Mark 14:62 may be cited as indicating that some
of these sayings belong to that period, but in this case they must
be interpreted in harmony with the declaration to Caiaphas.

(2) Matthew 10:23 suggests that most of these sayings belong
to the Galilean Ministry, that is, to a period when the Coming
of the Son of Man was thought to be imminent. Unfortunately,
no agreement has been reached among New Testament
scholars on the genuineness of this saying, and the tendency
is to regard it as unauthentic.

(3) If the sayings are early, it may well be that the communal
interpretation of the Son of Man was uppermost in the mind
of Jesus; in other words, by the coming of the Son of Man He
meant the establishing of the Elect Community to whom the

Kingdom is given. Without exegetical violence this meaning can be found in Luke 17:22, 24, 26, 30; in Luke 12:40 and 21:36; in Matthew 10:23, and possibly, but more doubtfully, in Luke 18:8b. Most of these sayings have to do with a 'day' or an 'hour,' and are in harmony with the dramatic announcement, 'The Rule of God is at hand,' with which Jesus began His Ministry and which the Twelve proclaimed during their campaign to the cities of Israel.

(4) There would be no difficulty in relating the stage of thought presumed above to those in which He applies the title 'Son of Man' to Himself, and, after Cæsarea Philippi, reinterprets it in terms of the idea of the Suffering Servant; for, in a manner strange to the modern man, the prophetic consciousness moves easily between the communal and personal aspects of great ideas. Even around the sayings relating to suffering, personal as they are, there is a communal aura, nor is the possibility excluded that the divine community was in His mind when He stood before Caiaphas.

What is urged above is not proof, but there is one further consideration which might turn the scale. Has criticism made enough of the Mission of the Twelve? The decisiveness of this event is hidden from the eyes of the ordinary reader of the Gospels because Mark 6:7, 12f. is a mere envelope enclosing the Mission Charge transmitted to the Evangelists in Mark, Q, M, and L. If we study the Charge itself, we cannot fail to be impressed by its dramatic character. 'The missionaries are to be like an invading army, and live on the country' (Manson, *Mission and Message of Jesus*, 473). Like Gehazi of old on his ministry of life and death (2 Kings 4:29), they are to salute no man by the way. Eating and drinking are secondary matters. The supreme business is to announce the speedy coming of the Kingdom. So tense is the feeling that during their absence Jesus sees in vision Satan fall like lightning from heaven (Luke 10:18). Is not the mission of the Twelve a dividing line as certain as Cæsarea Philippi itself? And to this degree was not Schweitzer right?

(1946)

X

A Great Text Reconsidered

ὃν προέθετο ὁ θεὸς ἱλαστήριον διὰ ῆ πίστεως ἐν τῷ αὐτοῦ αἵματι εἰς ἔνδειξιν τῆς δικαιοσύνης αὐτοῦ διὰ τὴν πάρεσιν τῶν προγεγονότων ἁμαρτημάτων ἐν τῇ ἀνοχῇ τοῦ θεοῦ, πρὸς τὴν ἔνδειξιν τῆς δικαιοσύνης αὐτοῦ ἐν τῷ νῦν καιρῷ, εἰς τὸ εἶναι αὐτὸν δίκαιον καὶ δικαιοῦντα τὸν ἐκ πίστεως Ἰησοῦ.—Romans 3:25f. (Westcott and Hort).

These words have played a great part in the history of Christian Doctrine; and for this reason it is very desirable that from time to time their meaning and interpretation should be reconsidered. Especially is this necessary since in contemporary discussions the passage is either neglected or is interpreted in ways which are open to challenge.

The rendering of the Authorized Version is as follows:

Whom God hath set forth to be a propitiation through faith in his blood, to declare his righteousness for the remission of sins that are past, through the forbearance of God; to declare, I say, at this time his righteousness: that he might be just, and the justifier of him which believeth in Jesus.

In the Revised Version several important changes were introduced. The phrase ἐν τῷ αὐτοῦ αἵματι was translated: 'by his blood,' and the words 'through faith' were enclosed by commas. The latter change was a great improvement, since in the teaching of St. Paul faith is always related to a person; it is out of harmony with New Testament teaching to speak of 'faith in his blood'. Among other changes made in the Revised Version the most important is the substitution of 'because of the passing over of the sins done aforetime' instead of 'for

127

the remission of the sins that are past,' as a rendering of the words: διὰ τὴν πάρεσιν τῶν προγεγονότων ἁμαρτημάτων. In this version the passage reads:

> Whom God set forth to be a propitiation, through faith, by his blood, to shew his righteousness, because of the passing over of the sins done aforetime, in the forbearance of God; for the shewing, I say, of his righteousness at this present season: that he might himself be just, and the justifier of him that hath faith in Jesus.

For 'set forth', the margin has 'purposed'; for 'to be a propitiation' 'to be propitiatory'; and for 'faith, by . . .' 'faith in his blood.' The effect of these changes is not only to render the Greek more closely, but also to bring the passage into greater accord with the 'traditional interpretation' of the text, the view, namely, that St. Paul saw in the sacrificial death of Jesus something which was necessary in order to demonstrate that God is righteous in His treatment of sin, and especially because the sins of past generations might be thought to have been overlooked or passed by in His forbearance.

In studying the words it is of great interest and importance to examine the modern translations of Dr. James Moffatt and Dr. C. A. Anderson Scott. Moffatt's translation is as follows:

> Whom God put forward as the means of propitiation by His blood, to be received by faith. This was to demonstrate the justice of God in view of the fact that sins previously committed during the time of God's forbearance had been passed over; it was to demonstrate His justice at the present epoch, showing that God is just Himself and that He justifies man on the score of faith in Jesus.

This translation is in line with the older interpretation indicated above, but this cannot be said of the translations offered by Dr. Anderson Scott in his *Christianity according to St. Paul* (1927), 72, in *The Abingdon Bible Commentary* (1929), 1144, and in his *Foot-Notes to St. Paul* (1935), 25. The third of these runs:

Whom God set forth, suffering unto blood, as one with power to reconcile through faith, with a view to the exhibition (=communication) of His righteousness, through the overlooking of past sins in the forbearance of God, with a view, I say, to the exhibition of His righteousness at this present time, that He may be at once Himself just and the justifier (= saviour) of him who founds on faith in Jesus.

In *Christianity according to St. Paul* ἐν τῷ αὐτοῦ αἵματι is rendered by 'dying a bloody death', ἱλαστήριον 'as one exercising reconciling power', and εἰς ἔνδειξιν 'with a view to conferring'. In the *Abingdon Bible* the corresponding renderings are: 'a victim unto blood', 'as one able to effect reconciliation', and 'unto the bestowal of', and διὰ τὴν πάρεσιν is translated 'with a view to the passing over'. Since the 'righteousness' of God is interpreted as 'an activity of God which reaches man in the form of salvation', the general effect of these renderings is to bring the passage into close agreement with the ideas of 2 Corinthians 5:19: 'God was in Christ reconciling the world unto himself.' The objective aspect of the sacrifice disappears, it is no longer a demonstration of the quality of righteousness in God, the overlooking of past sins is not the *cause* but the *purpose* of the Divine activity, and, as Dr. Scott explains, the sins in question are not those of past generations, but those of St. Paul and his contemporaries.[1] In a word, the passage explains 'how through the sacrifice of Christ men might become forgivable.'[2] Thus, the 'traditional interpretation' is not only abandoned, but reversed, and St. Paul is represented as saying the opposite of what most commentators have understood his words to mean.

In the present article I propose to examine the terminology and leading ideas of Romans 3:25f., and to endeavour to show that substantially the 'traditional interpretation' of the passage is correct.

---

[1] *Foot-Notes to St. Paul*, 27.

[2] *Christianity according to St. Paul*, 73.

I

It will be of advantage first to examine the meaning of the words and phrases.

προέθετο. The meaning of προτίθημι in the active and the middle is 'to set forth' or 'to set forth publicly'. In the middle it can also mean 'to set before oneself', 'propose', or 'purpose', as in Romans 1:13 and Ephesians 1:9. This meaning has been assigned to the verb in the present passage, but probably Sanday and Headlam are right in arguing that, in view of the many terms in the immediate context denoting publicity, the other rendering seems preferable.[1]

ἱλαστήριον. This rare word has been variously explained. A favourite opinion in ancient and modern times identifies it with the Hebrew *kapporeth*, the propitiatory or covering of the ark in the Holy of Holies. It is used in this sense in the LXX in Exodus 25:17, as a neuter adjective with the noun ἐπίθεμα (cover), and elsewhere (Exodus 31:7, etc.) with the article as a neuter substantive. The word has this meaning in Hebrews 9:5 (ὑπεράνω δὲ αὐτῆς Χερουβεὶν δόξης κατασκιάζοντα τὸ ἱλαστήριον). It should be recognized that in all these cases the rendering 'mercy-seat' (*Gnadenstuhl*) is misleading; it suggests a place where grace is dispensed, whereas, as Deissmann[2] has shown, the meaning is 'propitiatory cover' or 'propitiatory article'. It is improbable that the word is used with this reference in Romans 3:25. The article is wanting and the context does not suggest the idea; indeed, its introduction in the passage would be exceedingly abrupt and confused. In spite, therefore, of the strong support given to this interpretation by A. Ritschl[3] and many expositors,[4] it should be rejected.[5] On the basis of evidence from inscriptions Deissmann explains ἱλαστήριος as an adjective signifying 'of use for propitiation', and says that in Romans 3:25 it means 'propitiatory gift'.[6] B. Weiss[7] and others hold that it signifies 'means of propitiation'; others again

---

[1] *Romans I.C.C.*, 87.
[2] *Bible Studies*, 126f.
[3] *Die christliche Lehre von der Rechtfertigung und Versöhnung dargestellt*, ii. 171.
[4] Cf. Büchsel, *Theologisches Wörterbuch*, iii, 321f.
[5] Cf. Sanday and Headlam, *Romans I.C.C.* 87; Deissmann, *Bible Studies*, 124–9; H. A. W. Meyer, *Romans*, i. 171ff.
[6] *Op. cit.*, 130–3.
[7] Meyer, iv. 164f.

explain it as a neuter adjective, with θῦμα understood, in the sense of 'propitiatory sacrifice'.[1] On the whole, with Sanday and Headlam,[2] Denney,[3] and Anderson Scott,[4] it seems best to interpret the word more broadly, as a masculine adjective agreeing with ὄν in a predicative sense. If this view is taken, the best translation is 'means of expiation' or 'atonement'. For the rendering, 'as one with power to reconcile' (Anderson Scott) we should expect rather ἱλαστής or ἱλασκόμενος. In any case, the word does not suggest the appeasing or propitiating of God. C. H. Dodd's careful investigation of ἱλάσκεσθαι and its cognates has conclusively proved that, contrary to classical usage, these words are not used in the LXX as conveying this meaning, but 'the sense of performing an act whereby guilt or defilement is removed'.[5] Of Romans 3:25 he says: 'In any case the meaning conveyed (in accordance with LXX usage, which is constantly determinative for Paul), is that of expiation, not that of propitiation'.[6] More than this cannot be said until the relation of ἱλαστήριον to other words in the sentence is considered. For the moment it is enough to say that the meaning which is least open to objection is 'as a means of atonement'.

διὰ πίστεως. As already indicated this phrase should not be taken with ἐν τῷ αὐτοῦ αἵματι. It should be construed with ἱλαστήριον;[7] it is through the response of faith that Christ becomes the means of atonement. Little difference to the thought is made if the phrase is read in connexion with προέθετο.[8]

ἐν τῷ αὐτοῦ αἵματι. This phrase, which should also be taken either with ἱλαστήριον or with ὄν προέθετο . . . . ἱλαστήριον, is undoubtedly sacrificial in its significance. 'Like "Cross", "blood of Christ" is only another, more vivid expression for the death of Christ in its redemptive meaning.'[9] There is, I think, no justification for connecting the phrase with 'the

---

[1] Cf. Boylan, *Romans,* 58.
[2] *Romans, I.C.C.,* 88.
[3] *The Expositor's Greek Testament,* ii, 611.
[4] *Christianity according to St. Paul,* 68.
[5] *The Bible and the Greeks,* 93.
[6] *Op. cit.,* 94.
[7] Cf. F. Büchsel, *Theologisches Wörterbuch,* iii, 321.
[8] Cf. F. A. Philippi, *Romans,* i. 146.
[9] Cf. J. Behm, *Theologisches Wörterbuch,* i. 173.

overwhelming impress which Paul had received as a spectator of the Crucifixion',[1] and so for the renderings, 'suffering unto blood', or 'dying a bloody death'. The evidence that the Apostle was present at the Crucifixion is both slight and dubious. Moreover, we must interpret the phrase in line with New Testament usage, and with that of St. Paul in particular. When he speaks of 'being now justified by his blood' (Romans 5:9), he is clearly thinking of the life of Christ freely offered on behalf of men, and the same sacrificial meaning is to be found in 1 Corinthians 10:16, Ephesians 1:7; 2:13, and Colossians 1:20. The background of thought is the Old Testament principle that 'the blood is the life' (Genesis 9:4; Leviticus 17: 10–12; Deuteronomy 12:23).

εἰς ἔνδειξιν. This phrase expresses purpose, and since the noun means a 'showing forth' or 'proof', it must be rendered 'to shew' as in the Revised Version (Moffatt, 'to demonstrate'). There is no evidence to support the translation 'display so as to reach', in the sense of 'conveying' or 'communicating', proposed by Dr. Anderson Scott;[2] and the analogies he mentions, (ἐνεδείξατο in 2 Timothy 4:14, φανέρωσις in I Corinthians 12:7, and ἀπόδειξις in I Corinthians 2:4, together with the meaning of the Latin *exhibere* and its English equivalents), do not seem to me to supply this deficiency. It is not satisfactory to argue that, since St. Paul was not concerned as to the abstract righteousness of God, we may adopt an unattested meaning for ἔνδειξις when other unambiguous words lie ready to hand. On the contrary, we must take the word with its undoubted suggestion of 'demonstration' or 'proof',[3] and look with suspicion on the claim that St. Paul was not interested in the demonstration that God is righteous.[4]

τῆς δικαιοσύνης αὐτοῦ. Broadly speaking, we may say that in Pauline thought the 'righteousness of God' is not simply a quality possessed by Him, but is also, and at the same time, His saving activity amongst men; it is both what He is and what He gives.[5] In Romans 1:17 the latter thought is uppermost. God's righteousness is the gift of His grace to men. It is

---

[1] Anderson Scott, *Foot-Notes to St. Paul*, 25.

[2] *Chrisitianity according to St. Paul*, 71.

[3] Cf. 2 Corinthians 8:24: 'the proof of your love'; Philippians 1:28: 'an evident token of perdition,' 'a clear omen of ruin' (Moffatt).

[4] Anderson Scott, *op. cit.*, 71.

[5] See the valuable discussion of G. Schrenk, *Theologisches Wörterbuch*, ii. 205ff.

imparted 'to faith' (εἰς πίστιν), and 'on the ground of faith' (ἐκ πίστεως), and by it men live (cf. Habakkuk 2:4). The Old Testament basis for this thought is illustrated in passages in which 'righteousness' is closely associated with 'salvation' (e.g. Isaiah 46:13: 'I bring near my righteousness . . . . and my salvation shall not tarry'; cf. Isaiah 45:21; 51:5; Psalm 24:5). Even in Romans 1:17, however, the idea of righteousness as a *quality* of the divine action is not excluded. The use of ἀποκαλύπτεται ('is revealed'), rather than δίδοται or χαρίζεται, indicates that the righteousness in question is at the same time an attribute of the Divine nature. In Romans 3:25 it is probable that both ideas are also found, but here the thought of righteousness as a quality is more evident. The emphasis on 'faith' throughout the context (verses 22, 25f., 27, 30), as a basis or ground, strongly points to a righteousness which is received; but it seems perverse to limit the meaning of the term in Romans 3:25f. to this aspect. Indeed, of the two the idea of righteousness as a quality possessed by God is the more prominent. This is shown by the use of ἔνδειξις, the meaning of διὰ τὴν πάρεσιν (see below), and, above all, by the climax of the sentence in εἰς τὸ εἶναι αὐτὸν δίκαιον καὶ δικαιοῦντα. What God 'sets forth' in the work of Christ has for its goal the purpose that He may be righteous and at the same time declare righteous those who believe in Jesus. Whatever richer ideas there may be in St. Paul's use of the term, it must be firmly maintained that the righteousness described is 'the righteousness of God Himself'.[1]

---

[1] Cf. J. Denney, *The Expositor's Greek Testament*, ii. 612. Sanday and Headlam combine the two ideas well when they say: 'The righteousness of which the Apostle is speaking not only proceeds from God but *is* the righteousness of God Himself: it is this, however, not as inherent in the Divine Essence but as going forth and embracing the personalities of men' (*Romans I.C.C.*, 25). C. H. Dodd thinks that in St. Paul's religious vocabulary 'righteousness' is not only a moral attribute, but also (in accordance with Hebrew usage) stands for an act or activity; and he interprets Romans 1:17 as meaning: 'God is now seen to be vindicating the right, redressing wrong, and delivering men from the power of evil.' He thinks that 'righteousness' is used in the same sense in Romans 3:25f. 'Thus in order that God may be revealed as righteous it is necessary that He should be revealed as delivering men from the power of evil, as "justifying" them in the Old Testament sense of the word' (*The Moffatt N.T. Commentary: Romans*, 59). The truth of this statement cannot, I think, be gainsaid; but I do not think it in any way disposes of the claim that in Romans 3:25f., the main question at issue is whether God possesses the moral attribute of righteousness. The problem St. Paul is facing is whether God is both δίκαιος and ὁ δικαιῶν.

διὰ τὴν πάρεσιν. In Classical Greek the rare word πάρεσις is used with various meanings: 'dismissal', 'paralysis', 'remission' (of debts), 'neglect'. In the *Papyri* it is also used of the remission of punishment[1] and of debts.[2] In a famous discussion Archbishop Trench maintained that πάρεσις means a 'putting aside' of punishment as distinguished from ἄφεσις a 'putting away' or 'remission' of sins.[3] This meaning, which has the advantage of keeping close to the meaning of the verb παρίημι ('to pass by'), has been accepted by most commentators,[4] who render it by such phrases as 'passing by' or 'passing over'; but Lietzmann claims that 'the distinction between πάρεσις and ἄφεσις, possible in itself, is nowhere demonstrable, and is not here required.'[5] Bultmann also maintains that the two nouns have the same meaning.[6] Obviously, a decision on this point cannot be obtained by merely studying the meaning of the words; it is necessary also to take into account more general considerations and the context as a whole. When this is done, it seems to me that the balance of the argument is strongly in favour of translating πάρεσις by 'passing over'. (1) If St. Paul had been thinking of 'remission' or 'forgiveness', it would have been natural to use ἄφεσις as in Colossians 1:14 and Ephesians 1:7. The choice of the rarer word reflects a consciousness of a difference of meaning. (2) 'Passing over' is the more probable rendering if τῶν προγεγονότων ἁμαρτημάτων refers to the sins of former generations (see below). (3) If the noun is rendered 'remission', we must think of a purpose to be fulfilled, and, in consequence, understand διά *c. acc. prospectively*, with the meaning, 'with a view to'. This, while possible, seems to me most improbable; it is much more likely that διά *c. acc.* is used in its almost invariable *causal* sense, 'because of', with reference to something which has already happened. Instances of διά *c. acc.* with the meaning, 'with a view to', are extremely rare in Classical Greek; they are non-existent in the Septuagint, and are not mentioned by Moulton and Milligan in *The*

---

[1] Moulton and Milligan, *The Vocabulary of the Greek Testament*, 493.

[2] Deissmann, *Bible Studies*, 266.

[3] *Synonyms of the New Testament*, 110–16.

[4] So Sanday and Headlam, *Romans*, 90; H. A. W. Meyer, *Romans*, i. 177; R.V., Moffatt, etc.

[5] See Anderson Scott, *op. cit.*, 67.

[6] *Theologisches Wörterbuch*, i. 508.

Vocabulary of the Greek Testament.[1] The only possible New Testament example, apart from the present passage, is Romans 4:25: διὰ τὴν δικαίωσιν ἡμῶν, and in spite of the opinion of Sanday and Headlam,[2] it is extremely doubtful if this is an exception.[3] Taking all things into consideration, I think we are compelled to translate διὰ τὴν πάρεσιν, 'because of the passing over'.

τῶν προγεγονότων ἁμαρτημάτων. This phrase refers either to the sins of former generations or to those of the men of St. Paul's time.[4] In view of the strong emphasis on the present moment in the words, ἐν τῷ νῦν καιρῷ, the former seems preferable.

ἐν τῇ ἀνοχῇ τοῦ θεοῦ. The meaning of ἀνοχή (found also in Romans 2:4) is 'forbearance', 'suspense', 'delay'.[5] The preposition ἐν may be either temporal or indicates the motive. Sanday and Headlam[6] and H. A. W. Meyer[7] support the latter interpretation.

πρὸς τὴν ἔνδειξιν takes up the preceding phrase εἰς ἔνδειξιν. There is no significance in the change of preposition.

δίκαιον καὶ δικαιοῦντα: 'just and declaring just'.

τὸν ἐκ πίστεως Ἰησοῦ. An elliptical phrase well rendered by Anderson Scott, 'him who founds on Jesus'.

II

In summing up the results of the investigation, it seems to me that the probabilities are very strongly in favour of the 'traditional interpretation'. If we adopt the view that the passage explains how through the sacrifice of Christ men might become forgivable, we are compelled to accept a series of dubious lexical and grammatical expedients. We have to

---

[1] See the article of Douglas S. Sharp, the *Expository Times*, xxxix, 87–90. As classical examples of the prospective usage Mr. Sharp listed Thuc. iv. 40; Aristotle *Ethics*, iv. 3, 31; Plato, *Republic*, 524 C. My friend, Dr. W. F. Howard, has also pointed out to me an example in Polyb. ii. 56, 11–12.

[2] *Romans*, 116.

[3] If St. Paul had meant 'with a view to', he could easily have written: εἰς τὴν δικαίωσιν ἡμῶν. The awkwardness of the passage seems due to the semi-quotation of Isaiah 53:12 in 25a. What he means is that Christ was delivered up and raised because of our sins and our justification.

[4] Anderson Scott, *Foot-Notes to St. Paul*, 27.

[5] W. E. Wilson supports the translation 'delaying' with reference, not to punishment, but to the work of salvation, the *Expository Times*, xxix, 472.

[6] *Romans*, 90.　　[7] *Romans*, i. 178.

give to ἱλαστήριον a possible, but uncertain meaning; to deny the sacrificial significance of ἐν τῷ αὐτοῦ αἵματι; to attach to ἔνδειξις a rendering unattested elsewhere; to interpret the 'righteousness of God' in a sense which admirably suits its use in Second Isaiah, but does not appear to be the main thought in Romans; to translate πάρεσις as if St. Paul had used ἄφεσις; to assign to διά *c. acc.* a meaning, illustrated by a few classical examples, but not found in the LXX, the *Papyri*, and perhaps not even in Romans 4:25; and, finally, to deny a reference to past generations in contrast to the emphatic 'Now' in the phrase, ἐν τῷ νῦν καιρῷ. Some of these suggestions are possible, but when so many are concentrated in the space of two verses, it is permissible to suspect that the exegesis which they support is not St. Paul's thought. We are obtaining a meaning agreeable to modern thought at the expense of lexical and grammatical integrity.

The position is very different if we consider the 'traditional interpretation'. Admittedly, the rendering, 'means of atonement', or 'expiation', for ἱλαστήριον cannot be claimed as more than the best of several possibilities; but it is strongly supported by the phrase ἐν τῷ αὐτοῦ αἵματι and the meaning of ἱλάσκεσθαι in the Greek Bible. 'Passing over' is also not the only possible meaning of πάρεσις, but again it is supported by its derivation, the choice of the word in preference to ἄφεσις, and the backward reference of the immediate context. For the rest every word is used in its commonly accepted meaning, and there are no departures from what is normal in Hellenistic syntax. It is true that by this interpretation we obtain results which at first sight are less congenial to the modern mind, but in an attempt to elucidate the thought of an ancient writer this feature is irrelevant. It is conceivable also that our modern interpretations of the Atonement are feeble and unsatisfying. To the objection that the ideas found by the 'traditional interpretation' are not paralleled elsewhere in the Pauline Epistles, it is a sufficient reply that Romans is the most formal of St. Paul's writings, that in it the discussion of ultimate problems is to be expected, and that even in 3:25f. the Apostle does not work out fully his own thoughts. It is a glimpse, rather than an outline, of his theology that we obtain in this classical passage.

So far I have for convenience spoken of the 'traditional interpretation', but, of course, this general name covers various views, and it now remains to ask more closely what St. Paul's thought is.

Certain opinions may be ruled out forthwith. The passage in no way suggests that Christ died to appease the wrath of God; it does not teach a doctrine of vicarious punishment; nor does it present the Atonement as a transaction, the benefits of which are to be received passively. We must distinguish between the 'traditional interpretation' and later dogmatic ideas which have been associated with it.

The main question with which St. Paul is concerned is how God can be recognized as Himself righteous and at the same time as one who declares righteous believers in Christ.

It may be that St. Paul's doctrine of salvation had been assailed by Jews who asserted that it was inconsistent with a belief in God's righteousness. It may also be that the problem is only one which had presented itself to the Apostle's mind. The point of difficulty is really modern as well as ancient; it arises from the contemplation of the Cross as an event at a particular time in human history. What is to be said of His action or want of action in previous generations?

St. Paul's answer is not complete, but there is every reason to think that this is the question which confronted him. His answer is twofold. First, God has shown Himself to be righteous in the fact that in Christ He had met the moral situation created by sin. He had confronted men with a means of expiation or atonement, operative in Christ and His sacrificial death, and effective in men in virtue of the faith-relationship between them and Him. The living way was open. There it stood, and because of it God was a righteous God and a justifying God. Secondly, His attitude to the pre-Christian world had been one of forbearance and mercy. If He had appeared to pass over sins done aforetime, this was because He was long-suffering and merciful, and the proof of this was His ultimate and decisive action in Christ. It is no sufficient objection to this interpretation to say that in Romans 1 St. Paul describes in the strongest terms the punishment which inevitably falls upon sin and that, therefore, he could not have thought or spoken of the 'passing-over' of sins. He does so speak in the words, διὰ τὴν πάρεσιν τῶν προγεγονότων ἁμαρτημάτων. We must therefore be bold enough to draw the conclusion that he did not regard punishment as an adequate way of meeting the problem of sin. Punished though men might be, the moral situation had not been met. The stronger objection is that the difficulty is not fully met by his reference to the Divine forbearance, though we must not miss the suggestion of a Divine Love which waits for better things, unwilling to believe that hope is vain. The force of this objection must be frankly admitted. Perhaps the refusal to do this explains why Romans 3:25f. has so often been placed on the rack. St. Paul must be self-consistent at all costs, even at the expense of grammar! The truer exegesis is to recognize an uncompleted element in his attempt to solve a supreme problem of faith.

It is germane to the inquiry to consider how this part of the problem might have been treated. Several suggestions present themselves, and it is satisfying to find that they emerge elsewhere in St. Paul's writings. One is the thought that the saving work of God can only be displayed at a particular time in history, 'in the fulness of the time', which can be known to God alone (cf. Galatians 4:4). Another truth is that the work of Christ is racial and representative; and this thought St. Paul begins to work out in Romans 5:12–21, but is turned aside by his desire to insist that the free gift in Christ out-spans the trespass in Adam (Romans 5:15). A third suggestion, that the faith-relation is not subject to the limitations of mortal life, he does not make at all, except in so far as he approaches it in his hope of the restoration of Israel in Romans 11, and his plea that 'the gifts and the calling of God are without repentance' (Romans 11:29).

Finally, it may be noted that in his opening statement there are also rich thoughts left undeveloped. He asserts that the death of Christ shows that God is righteous, but beyond the hints conveyed in ἱλαστήριον, ἐν τῷ αὐτοῦ αἵματι, and διὰ πιστέως he does not tell us how this proof is made. The language used is enough to show that his thought is moving in sacrificial channels. None the less, it fails to come to full expression. Why is this the case? Why does he select a word so suggestive and yet so ambiguous as ἱλαστήριον?

The answer is that, for all his use of sacrificial language, he has not entered into the spiritual significance of the cultus as his younger contemporary, the *auctor ad Hebraeos*, entered. He is an ardent mission-preacher and an original thinker, not a philosophical theologian. Further, his emphasis upon the thought that it is *God* who set forth Christ as ἱλαστήριον makes it difficult to work out here the *Godward* reference implicit in his own terminology. That we are justified in saying that such a reference is implicit is shown not merely by the terminology but by his emphasis elsewhere on the racial and representative ministry of Christ (Romans 5:12–21). And if we ask what is the votive-gift of Christ, in virtue of which He is the 'means of atonement', the answer, developed along Pauline lines, is that it lies in His obedience (Romans 5:19), appropriated by faith (Romans 3:25f.), sacramental communion (1 Corinthians 10:16), and sacrificial living (Colossians 1:24; Romans 12:1).

(*1939*)

A list of the published writings of Vincent Taylor

Compiled by Owen E. Evans

ABBREVIATIONS

ET	*Expository Times*
HJ	*Hibbert Journal*
JTS	*Journal of Theological Studies*
LQHR	*London Quarterly & Holborn Review*
NTS	*New Testament Studies*

1919

Is the Lukan Narrative of the Birth of Christ a Prophecy? (ET 30, 377–8)

1920

The Historical Evidence for the Virgin Birth (Oxford, the Clarendon Press)

1922

Proto-Luke (ET 33, 250–2)

1925

The Value of the Proto-Luke Hypothesis (ET 36, 476–7)

A Cry from the Siege: A Suggestion Regarding a Non-Markan Oracle Embedded in Lk. XXI. 20–36 (JTS 26, 136–144)

The Lukan Authorship of the Third Gospel and the Acts (*The Expositor*, Ninth Series, 282–291)

1926

Behind the Third Gospel: A Study of the Proto-Luke Hypothesis (Oxford, the Clarendon Press)

The Alleged Neglect of M. Alfred Loisy (HJ 24, 563–72)

1927

The First Draft of St. Luke's Gospel (S.P.C.K.)
Professor Strömholm's Riddle (HJ 25, 285–98)
The Fourth Gospel and Some Recent Criticism (HJ 25, 725–43)

1928

Is the Proto-Luke Hypothesis Sound? (JTS 29, 147–55)
The Psychology of the Johannine Christ-testimonies (HJ 27, 123–37)

1930

The Gospels: a Short Introduction (Epworth Press)
Recent Foreign Theology: Jesus and History (ET 41, 477)
National Contributions to Biblical Science: The Contribution of France to New Testament Science (ET 42, 76–81)
The Mandaeans and the Fourth Gospel (HJ 28, 531–46)

1931

Reunion and Non-conformity (HJ 29, 595–608)

1932

The Barthian School: Rudolf Bultmann (ET 43, 485–90)

1933

The Formation of the Gospel Tradition (Macmillan)

1934

The Message of the Epistles: Second Peter and Jude (ET 45, 437–41)
Some Outstanding New Testament Problems: Introduction (ET 46, 17–18)
Some Outstanding New Testament Problems: The Elusive Q (ET 46, 68–74)
M. Loisy on the Birth of Christianity: A Reply (HJ 33, 22–36)

1935

Professor J. M. Creed and the Proto-Luke Hypothesis (ET 46, 236–8)
Professor Creed's Rejoinder (ET 46, 379)

Recent Foreign Theology: R. Otto's *Reich Gottes und Menschensohn* (ET 46, 282–3)

Some Outstanding New Testament Problems: Epilogue (ET 47, 72–6)

From Tradition to Gospel (LQHR, Sixth Series 4, 145–55)

1936

'The Synoptic Problem' in *Supplement to Peake's Commentary* (T.C. and E.C. Jack)

Recent Foreign Theology: J. L. Nuelsen's *Die Ordination im Methodismus* (ET 47, 429–30)

1937

Jesus and His Sacrifice: A Study of the Passion-Sayings in the Gospels (Macmillan)

'The Spirit in the New Testament' in *The Doctrine of the Holy Spirit* (Headingley Lectures, Epworth Press)

The Best Books on the Atonement (ET 48, 267–73)

1938

Recent Foreign Theology: The Lord's Supper (ET 49, 427–8)

After Fifty Years: The Gospel and the Gospels (ET 50, 8–12)

1939

Great Texts Reconsidered: Romans 3, 25f. (ET 50, 295–300)

Constructive Theology: Forgiveness (ET 51, 16–21)

'Jesus and His Sacrifice': A Rejoinder (LQHR, Sixth Series 8, 45–55)

1940

The Atonement in New Testament Teaching (The Fernley-Hartley Lecture, Epworth Press)

1941

Forgiveness and Reconciliation: A Study in New Testament Theology (Macmillan)

Is it possible to write a Life of Christ? Some aspects of the Modern Problem (ET 52, 60–5)

1943

The Proto-Luke Hypothesis: A Rejoinder (ET 54, 219–22)
The Passion Sayings (ET 54, 249–50)

1946

The 'Son of Man' Sayings Relating to the Parousia (ET 58, 12–15)

1947

The Unity of the New Testament: The Doctrine of the Atonement (ET 58, 256–9)

1948

Unsolved New Testament Problems: The Messianic Secret in Mark (ET 59, 146–51)

1949

Unsolved New Testament Problems: The Apocalyptic Discourse of Mark XIII (ET 60, 94–8)
The Creative Element in the Thought of Jesus (LQHR, Sixth Series 18, 109–17)

1950

Loisy's 'Origins of the New Testament' (HJ 48, 339–47)

1951

'The Life and Ministry of Jesus' in *The Interpreter's Bible*, Vol. 7, 114–44 (Abingdon Press)
Living Issues in Biblical Scholarship: The Church and the Ministry (ET 62, 269–74)

1952

The Gospel According to St. Mark: The Greek Text with Introduction, Notes and Indexes (Macmillan)

1953

The Names of Jesus. First Series of the Speaker's Lectures in the University of Oxford (Macmillan)
Doctrine and Evangelism (Epworth Press)
The Apostolic Gospel: Our Message for 1953, being a Paper read at the Ministerial Session of the Methodist Conference at Preston, 23rd July 1952 (Epworth Press)

'Wilbert Francis Howard 1880–1952' in The Proceedings of the
   British Academy, Volume XLV (London: Oxford University
   Press)
The Order of Q (JTS, New Series 4, 27–31)

1954

The Life and Ministry of Jesus. Second Series of the Speaker's
   Lectures in the University of Oxford (Macmillan)
Important and Influential Foreign Books: Introduction
   (ET 65, 166–8)
Important and Influential Foreign Books: W. Wrede's *The
   Messianic Secret in the Gospels* (ET 65, 246–50)

1955

The Epistle to the Romans. Epworth Preacher's Commentaries
   (Epworth Press)
Important Hypotheses Reconsidered: An Introductory Article
   (ET 66, 359–61)
Important Hypotheses Reconsidered: The Proto-Luke Hypo-
   thesis (ET 67, 12–16)
Dr. Henry G. Meecham (ET 67, 41–2)
The Origin of the Markan Passion-sayings (NTS 1, 159–67)

1956

The Cross of Christ: Eight Lectures delivered at Drew University
   (Macmillan)
Sources of the Lukan Passion Narrative (ET 68, 95)

1957

The Messianic Secret in Mark: A Rejoinder to the Rev. Dr.
   T. A. Burkill (HJ 55, 241–8)

1958

The Person of Christ in New Testament Teaching. Part III of the
   Speaker's Lectures in the University of Oxford (Macmillan)
The State of New Testament Studies Today (LQHR, Sixth
   Series 27, 81–6)

1959

'The Original Order of Q' in A. J. B. Higgins ed., *New Testament
   Essays: Studies in Memory of T. W. Manson 1893–1958*
   (Manchester University Press)

Professor Oscar Cullmann's 'Die Christologie des Neuen Testaments' (ET 70, 136—40)

Milestones in Books (ET 70, 231–3)

Modern Issues in Biblical Studies: Methods of Gospel Criticism (ET 71, 68–72)

The New Testament Origins of Holy Communion (LQHR, Sixth Series 28, 84–90)

1960

Religious Certainty (ET 72, 15–18 and 49–52)

1961

The Text of the New Testament: a Short Introduction (Macmillan)

1962

Does the New Testament call Jesus 'God'? (ET 73, 116–8)

Theologians of our Time: Heinz Schürmann (ET 74, 77–81)

The Narrative of the Crucifixion (NTS 8, 333–4)

1963

Theologians of our Time: Friedrich Rehkopf (ET 74, 262–6)

1964

Rehkopf's List of Words and Phrases Illustrative of Pre-Lukan Speech Usage (JTS, New Series 15, 59–62)

Second Thoughts: Formgeschichte (ET 75, 356–8)

Life after Death: The Modern Situation (ET 76, 76–9)